23·99
✓

D0524029

Respecting C

HMC
LEARNING
CENTRE

WITHDRAWN

Rother Valley Campus

0051364

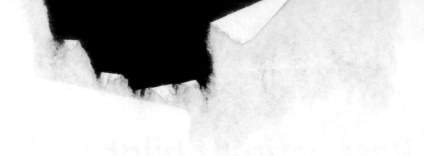

Also available from Continuum

Childhood and the Philosophy of Education, Andrew Stables
Children as Decision Makers in Education, Sue Cox, Anna Robinson-Pant,
   Caroline Dyer and Michele Schweisfurth
Children's Futures, Paul Croll, Carol Fuller and Gaynor Attwood
Right to Childhoods, Dimitra Hartas
Whose Childhood Is It, Richard Eke, Helen Butcher and Mandy Lee
Working Together for Children, Gary Walker

New Childhoods Series:
Rethinking Childhood, Phil Jones
Rethinking Children and Families, Nick Frost
Rethinking Children and Research, Mary Kellet
Rethinking Children, Violence and Safeguarding, Lorraine Radford
Rethinking Children's Communication, Alison Clark
Rethinking Children's Rights, Sue Welch and Phil Jones

Respecting Childhood

Tim Loreman

FMC
EARNING
CENTRE

continuum

Continuum International Publishing Group

The Tower Building   80 Maiden Lane
11 York Road   Suite 704
London SE1 7NX   New York NY 10038

www.continuumbooks.com

© Tim Loreman 2009

All rights reserved. No part of this publication may be reproduced
or transmitted in any form or by any means, electronic or mechani-
cal, including photocopying, recording, or any information storage
or retrieval system, without prior permission in writing from the
publishers.

Author has asserted his right under the Copyright, Designs and Patents
Act, 1988, to be identified as Author of this work.

British Library Cataloguing-in-Publication Data
A catalogue record for this book is available from the British Library.

ISBN: 978-08264-3244-5 (paperback)
      978-08264-3370-1 (hardcover)

Library of Congress Cataloging-in-Publication Data
A catalog record of this book is available from the Library of Congress.

Typeset by Newgen Imaging Systems Pvt Ltd, Chennai, India
Printed and bound in Great Britain by Athenaeum Press Ltd., Gateshead, Tyne & Wear

APR 15
0051364
305.23 LOR

For my own children,
Holly and Tom, and my wife, Lizz,
with love.

Contents

viii Contents

Acknowledgements

I am grateful for the love, support, patience, and assistance of my wife, Lizz, who read every page of the manuscript and provided invaluable suggestions for improvement. I would also like to thank my two children, Tom and Holly, for helping me to see what is important in the life of a child, and for providing me with the motivation to share those ideas with others. To my extended family: Mum, Dad, Eleanor, Paul, Suzanne, William, Isabella, Chris, and Elliot. Thanks for your support, love, and encouragement.

Further, I would like to thank my editor, Joanne Allcock, for her enthusiasm for the project and her guidance. Thanks to my friend Tim Labron and my other colleagues and friends at Concordia University College of Alberta.

Preface

This book offers a critical examination of modern-day views and practices related to children and childhood. Broadbent (2006) remarked that we live in a culture of complaint, in which there is a tendency to complain about what is wrong without necessarily concerning ourselves with what is positive and what is working well (see also Loreman, 2007a). The logical extension of this is that perhaps one should not criticize for fear of being viewed as negative or unproductive. This text challenges that idea, and is written with the belief that criticism is valuable because it helps in identifying areas in which improvement is needed. Criticism, however, does not have to end there. At times this text suggests possibilities, alternatives to the status quo where they exist, and ways of moving forward that are respectful to children and childhood. Sometimes, however, a simple critique is offered without proposing a solution. In both instances, the intent is to provide a vehicle and catalyst for reflection and discussion. Hopefully this book will in some measure contribute to the promotion of positive views and practices for working with children.

Much of the literature in this area to date, while making a critical contribution to our understanding of conceptualizations of children and childhood, has been either written for a different audience using complex terminology and structure, has provided different insights into a narrow range of topics related to childhood, or has not followed an evidence-based approach in supporting the arguments made (see e.g. a review by Derevensky, 2008). One of the goals of this text is to provide a broad, plain-language, but scholarly, and above all evidence-based overview of the topic. Building on the work of previous authors, this book draws on a variety of research, literature, and examples to support the arguments it contains, and is structured in such a way as to target and examine the major elements of the life of a child. Of course, a book of this length could not possibly cover all of the elements of childhood in a comprehensive way. Instead, specific areas have been chosen which serve to describe the key issues involved within the broader topics. While bias is acknowledged (few, if any, works are bias free), this text has attempted to examine both sides of most arguments as they are evident in the research and scholarly literature.

It is helpful at the outset to define the scope of this text. What exactly is meant by the term 'childhood', and to what does the term 'society' refer? When scrutinized these are found to be nebulous and fluid concepts. What constitutes a child has evolved throughout history, and is complicated by legislative definitions which can vary from nation to nation. One of the most succinct definitions comes from Greenleaf (1978) who defines childhood as being the absence of adulthood. This simple definition is helpful in that it is sensitive to context and individual difference. If a person is commonly and persistently engaging in thinking and activities normally associated with adults in a particular society, then they are no longer a child. For some this can occur at a very young chronological age, while for others it will take much longer. As a general rule of thumb, in western society people of the ages 17 or 18 are unlikely to still be children, while most people at the age of 14 would be. This is a fairly arbitrary designation of ages, but perhaps helpful to envisage when the absence of childhood begins to occur, at least in the context of the scope of this text.

The term society is in some respects more difficult to define. In this text the term is used is used to define broad social contexts such as nations or large regions. The *Merriam Webster Online Dictionary* defines society as 'a community, nation, or broad grouping of people having common traditions, institutions, and collective activities and interests' (Sec 3b). Further, when the term society is used in this text it is generally in reference to western society. This does not mean that the discussion or relevance of the book pertains only to western countries, but rather that the ideas and examples discussed can generally be linked to a westernized cultural heritage or background, even if these ideas can also be found traditionally, or have been more recently adopted, in other regions (such as can be seen in the Case Study of Taiwan in Chapter 2, where western ideas about studying hard have supported similar pre-existing eastern ideas to produce the circumstances in that region of the world). The term society in this text means large groupings of people in places in the world which are influenced by, or in agreement with, western cultural norms and values. This is an imperfect definition, but one which will enable discussion and examination of the various issues in this book.

Most chapters in this book are divided into three broad sections. The first section deals with the topic in the context of society at large. The second section deals with the topic in the context of the home life of the child (or other similar out-of-school contexts), and the third deals with the topic in the school context. These three broad areas have been chosen because they are important cultural contexts, and represent the environments in which most children spend a considerable amount of their lives.

Chapter 1 provides a basic introduction into what is to follow in other chapters of the book. It sets the tone for the text through a brief examination of modern views of childhood and how these came to be. In doing so it orients the reader to the main issues and lays a foundation for the more specific topics to follow.

Chapter 2 is concerned with time. It examines children's present and future, and how children are allowed and encouraged to use that time. It argues that adults are too often involved in over-structuring children's time, and requiring them to use it in ways which are disrespectful to the stage of childhood. The argument is made for a reduction in the emphasis on looking to the future in favour of respecting the present and immediate experience of childhood.

Chapter 3 examines relationships and family life, with a particular emphasis on how adults have conspired to disrupt and devalue those relationships. It examines notions of child independence and individuality, along with some of the concerns surrounding child-rearing advice found in the popular psychology media, and the impact of increased use of technology in society.

Chapter 4 examines children's capacities and abilities and how these have been devalued and disrespected, especially throughout the positivist twentieth-century up to the present day. It discusses elitist and inappropriate practices for learning, along with limiting and impoverished school curricula.

Chapter 5 is concerned with issues of power and control, and how these impact views and practices relating to the behaviour of children. The nature of childhood morality, corporal punishment, parenting styles, classroom management techniques, and views of child behaviour that have come down to us through history are examined.

Chapter 6 discusses children's differences, particularly in relation to social constructions of difference (including disability, race, gender, religion, sexual orientation, and social) and how those constructs impact the way we work and live with children. The marginalization of these groups is discussed. Views of difference and types of discrimination on that basis are outlined.

Chapter 7 concludes by presenting the case for a way forward towards a more respectful way of viewing, living, and working with children based on a balanced, pragmatic approach, and common sense.

This text contains a variety of pedagogical features. Each chapter (with the exception of Chapters 1 and 7) begins with a *concept map* of the ideas to be discussed in that chapter. Some of the bubbles on each concept map are intentionally left blank in recognition of the complexity, depth, and ultimate impossibility of providing the reader with any more than a framework of each topic.

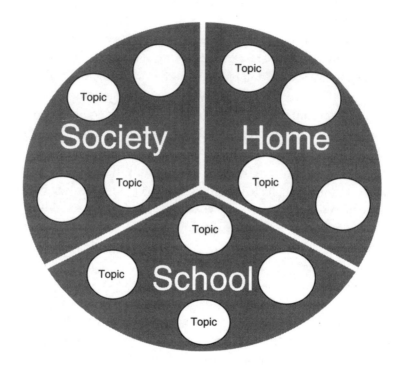

'Windows on Research' are intended to provide the reader with examples of the sort of research that has informed the various aspects of each chapter. They provide a time-out from the main body of the text, and an opportunity to engage with more narrowly focused studies in the context of this more general treatment. Most chapters also contain more conventional pedagogical features such as a Case Study, Discussion Questions, and a list of Further Resources. These can be used together or separately by individuals or groups as catalysts for further dialogue and exploration of each topic.

University instructors adopting this book as a class text may find benefit in having students read a chapter per week (or whatever time frame suits), and devoting class time to discussion of the various ideas presented, using the pedagogical features as tools for enrichment of classroom activities. Readers not using this text for the purposes of formal study may simply wish to read the text and use the pedagogical features as prompts for personal reflection. There is no right or wrong way to use this book. Whichever way one chooses to use it, the hope is that it will provide an enjoyable and productive read.

Introduction 1

Childhood is often remembered by those no longer in it as a carefree, happy time; a time for exploration, for discovery, and for satisfying one's curiosity. Yet childhood has come under strain as a result of demands made by the very same adults. Instead of being viewed as a stage of life worthy of respect in its own right, with its own unique features, it is now too often viewed as disconnected from important human endeavours, or at best as preparation for the future. This is evidenced in parenting styles, practices and structures in schools, media representations, and other practices and views held by adults. As a result of these views, many disrespectful ways of living and working with children have been proposed and adopted. The central thesis of this book is that what is needed is a more balanced approach to working and living with children, which is based on a respectful view of children and childhood. It calls for actions and views of children which allow them to be children, and to live out their childhood in the present, rather than having to follow the dubious proposition of maximizing learning and development in order to become more competitive and successful adults in the future.

This chapter provides a rationale for the main ideas featured throughout the book, and serves as an advance organizer for themes discussed in the other chapters. It outlines some of the background reasons as to why children are viewed, treated, and educated in the way they are in modern society.

The rationale for this text

In order to know what it is to respect childhood, the constituent elements and main features of this stage of life must first be understood. Pridmore

(2007) notes that nineteenth-century fantasy writer George MacDonald regarded

> childhood not so much as a stage in life to be left behind but as a condition to which to aspire. He [saw] in childhood an attunement, both with nature and with the nature of things, and a sharp awareness of 'the other and the beyond'. He [held] that these are not transient characteristics, features of a passing phase of life. They belong rather to our fulfilled humanity, to our well-being at any age. Thus, childhood becomes a continuing moral and spiritual goal. (p. 61)

Childhood is a unique stage of life in which humans are not only growing physically, but are also learning at an astonishing rate with sharpened cognitive abilities compared to adults (Richards, Shipley, Fuhrer, & Wadsworth, 2004). It is a joyful time of energy and enthusiasm, one in which the world becomes an experimental laboratory with learning occurring through play, as children construct knowledge about the world in which they live (Molland, 2004; Sprung, 2003; Vygotsky, 1978).

Another central feature of childhood is an active and creative imagination. This is so well known that it has become a virtual cliché. It is, nonetheless, true. Young children especially believe that magic is real and tangible (Tsukakoshi, 2007). Their lives in the real world become enmeshed and entangled in their magical fantasy world, enabling them to live in both. This is evident in the field of study of childhood imaginary friendships, which describes children playing with their pretend friends in contexts adults might consider to be real world (Klausen & Passman, 2007). Further, the presence of imaginary friends is not limited only to young children; a relationship with the fantasy world continues throughout childhood (Pearson et al., 2001; Prinsen & Hellendorn, 1989).

Childhood, like all other stages of life, is also a time in which relationships are important. Following Bronfenbrenner's (1979) model, children form the strongest relationships initially with those closest to them, generally their immediate caregivers. As children grow and develop, their relationships fan out in incremental stages to include stronger relationships with the extended family unit, friends, and finally other members of society more distant to their immediate caregivers. The importance of meaningful relationships with those in a child's life is evident in the wide variety of research literature dealing with the consequences to a child's life of poor relationships, and the development of research instruments aimed at investigating the nature of child social relationships (Zlatka, 2007).

Respect for childhood

Any attempt to better respect childhood, then, must at its heart be directed at preserving these unique characteristics, among others. The idea of respecting childhood likely means many things to many people, so it is useful to define exactly what it means in the context of this text. The remainder of this book addresses topics which directly relate and contribute to the following definition of what it is to respect childhood. Respecting childhood means:

- to provide children with the basic necessities of life outlined in the United Nations Declaration on the Rights of the Child (1959) and the United Nations International Convention on the Rights of the Child (1989)
- to value children's time, especially the present
- to value children's enjoyment of childhood
- to value children's relationships with others
- to value children's contributions to family and society
- to value children's individuality and diversity
- to value and accept children's abilities and capacities.

Window on Research

Gleeson and Hohmann (2006) conducted a study examining the friendship concepts of 84 children between 3 and 5 years using a verbally administered questionnaire and interviews. The study examined friendships in terms of social provisions (the social benefits of friendship) which included companionship, intimacy, reliable alliance (being there when needed), affection, and enhancement of worth. The study found that reciprocal friends (where two children cite one another as being friends) and imaginary friends were the best sources of social provisions, followed by unilateral friends (a friendship identified by only one child) and non-friendship. This study not only demonstrates the importance of reciprocal friendships for young children, but also the social provisions that imaginary friends can provide for children, which in this study were equal to real friendships.

The image of the child in society

Adults often conceptualize children in very negative ways, viewing their unique characteristics as substandard or in need of improvement. The word immature has come to have negative connotations associated with it, and adults admonish children for acting immature when they want to express their disapproval for a particular behaviour. Immaturity implies a state of transition, and if we accept this then all children are by definition immature in most respects if compared with adults. When one speaks of immaturity and childhood, however, one is speaking of two very different things. If childhood is seen as a stage with its own unique characteristics which are to be valued in their own right, then this is not transitional immaturity, but rather a distinct period of life. If one values childhood, why would a rush towards mature behaviour be desirable? There is much about childhood to commend it, and if it is simply seen as a transitional period of life then ideas about childhood and practices for working with children take on a negative, deficit-based tone. A brief look at how children have been viewed with respect to their education provides a good lens though which to think about wider conceptualizations about childhood.

A negative view of children: Traditional foundations

Figure 1.1 lists some of the ways in which children are conceptualized by adults in society, and these conceptualizations are reflected in many education systems. Some of these elements have a long tradition of thought behind them, but are nonetheless disrespectful towards children. Many of these elements are discussed in depth in other chapters in this book, and some of these themes in relation to children with disabilities have been touched on in a previous work (Loreman, 2007a); however, it is worthwhile to spend a short amount of time here considering these ideas.

Many ideas noted in Figure 1.1 have historical and traditional roots. In his fictional novel *The Clergyman's Daughter*, George Orwell (1935) describes a classroom where children are treated according to how much their parents

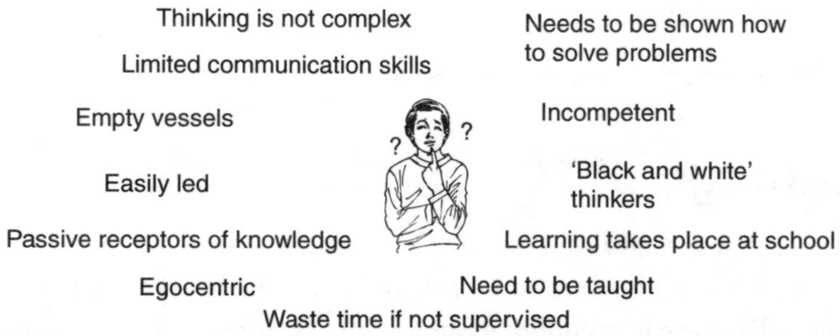

Thinking is not complex
Limited communication skills

Needs to be shown how
to solve problems

Empty vessels

Incompetent

Easily led

'Black and white'
thinkers

Passive receptors of knowledge

Learning takes place at school

Egocentric

Need to be taught

Waste time if not supervised

Figure 1.1 Some conceptions of the child

can pay in tuition, and learning is given a secondary consideration. Orwell himself was a teacher for a short period of time and must have experienced similar situations. Children are taught through drill and practice, as though they are empty vessels. This idea that children come to us to be filled with knowledge is a traditional view of children, conceptualized by Locke in the seventeenth century, however it still has currency today. Locke, influenced by the Enlightenment thinking of his time, believed in the existence of objective bodies of knowledge; undeniable universal facts waiting to become known through using scientific process and reason, which in his view would form the basis of any sound educational programme (Tarcov, 1984). In Orwell's book, children are expected to receive knowledge in a more or less passive manner, not being trusted to learn in a social or active way. Indeed, when the teacher attempts to indulge children's interests, she is quickly told to revert back to the old methods. The children are strictly disciplined (being naturally naughty), and their days are filled with meaningless copying and recitation so as to keep them occupied. Many of our parents and grandparents grew up in environments such as these, where high levels of order and control were put into place so as to keep children from doing the wrong things. When consideration is given to how negatively children have been viewed throughout the centuries (see Greenspan, 1978), it is no surprise that by the early twentieth century views of childhood had degenerated to that level.

These views of children persist to this day. We see them evident in much of the drill and practice teaching that occurs in classrooms. Children still regularly engage in rote learning of meaningless lists of words which they may never actually use in their writing in order to pass spelling tests, they still chant their multiplication tables, and school curricula throughout the world continues to maintain a strong focus of learning a series of facts. The maintenance of discipline in the classroom, while usually lacking the physical punishments of the past, has become known as classroom management. This amounts to the employment of strategies which help to ensure that children behave in ways approved of by the teacher, still the sole authority figure in most classrooms. Schools are not necessarily to blame for working with children in this way; they tend to reflect the values and expectations of adults in society.

Positive views of children: An example from Reggio Emilia, Italy

An example of an educational system in which a positive image of the child has been adopted comes from the municipal early childhood education

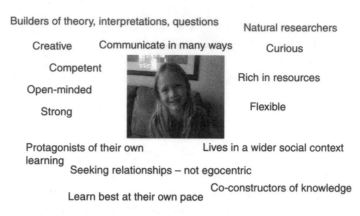

Builders of theory, interpretations, questions   Natural researchers

Creative   Communicate in many ways   Curious

Competent

Open-minded   Rich in resources

Strong   Flexible

Protagonists of their own   Lives in a wider social context
learning
Seeking relationships – not egocentric

Co-constructors of knowledge
Learn best at their own pace

Figure 1.2 The image of the child in Reggio Emilia

system in Reggio Emilia, Italy (Figure 1.2). This system, widely regarded as an international beacon of excellence in early childhood education, bases its entire educational approach on the premise that children are rich in resources, capacities, abilities, and intelligence in all its different forms.

Educators in Reggio Emilia tend to view children in the context of their relationships with family, friends, professionals, and the community. The child is seen as inseparable from these relationships that must be valued and nurtured. They also hold positive views of children in other ways; they see them as competent, active learners, and protagonists of their own learning. Children are not empty vessels waiting to be filled. They come to learning with any number of capacities, skills, talents, and abilities, and they apply those in their endeavours to socially construct knowledge (Loreman, 2007a; Rinaldi, 2006). In short, they are rich in personal resources, and with the guidance of a sensitive teacher, apply these resources to learning. Children are seen as being able to communicate their learning in many ways (not just written and verbal), and all are viewed as valid ways of making learning visible (Malaguzzi, 1998).

In the same way that educational systems with more traditional views of children reflect the values and beliefs evident in those societies and communities, so too does the educational system of Reggio Emilia. Reggio Emilia has a strong community identity, with traditionally left-wing political sympathies and a unique history of people working together within the context of supporting and valuing the individual. This is reflected in their early education system. Like-minded educators in Reggio Emilia and around the world would like to see the adoption of this systemic valuing of the competent child become more widespread, however there is a recognition that there is still much work to be done on the international level in order to achieve this. According to Rinaldi (2006)

> Much has been said and written about the competent child (who has the ability to learn, love, be moved, and live), the child who has a wealth of potentials, the powerful child in relation to what s/he is and can be right from birth. In practice, however, very little has been done which takes this image seriously. (p. 105; also cited in Loreman, 2007a)

This chapter has provided an introduction to the major themes to follow in this book. Each chapter from this point forward will endeavour to build a case for the adoption of more respectful views and practices relating to children.

Window on Research

Koyama, Takahashi, and Mori (2006) conducted a study on adult perceptions of children's cuteness in a Japanese setting. They asked 84 childless undergraduate students and 72 adults who had one or more children to watch short films of two 5-year-old children of different genders dressed in 'boyish' or 'girlish' clothes, and playing at dressing in clothes typically associated with the opposite gender. The participants then used a 43-item questionnaire to assess the cuteness of the children. The questionnaire was developed on the basis of a qualitative pilot study in which participants described situations they thought were cute involving children aged 3 to 6. Four aspects of cuteness were identified and incorporated into the questionnaire. These included childlike behaviour in general, physical cuteness, children's behaviour in pretending to be adults, and adults' protective feelings towards children.

The study found some differences between responses of the childless group and the group with children, as well as some differences depending on the gender of the child. However, both groups of participants rated the factor of childlike behaviour as having the most impact on their perceptions of cuteness. Physical cuteness seemed to be a more important factor in assessing overall cuteness for girls than boys.

Case Study: Tony's Story

On the recommendation of a friend, 3-year-old Tony's parents decided to get his speech tested by a speech-language pathologist. He was having difficulty articulating some words, and his vocabulary seemed limited for his age. His parents were surprised to discover that according to the tests, his receptive language was on the second percentile, and his expressive language was on the fourth percentile

Case Study—cont'd

compared to other 3-year-olds. On the suggestion of the speech-language patholo-gist, Tony was tested by an occupational therapist who was asked to check for any possible oral-motor difficulties. On the basis of these assessments, Tony qualified for special early intervention funding from the government.

At a meeting to discuss the test results and develop a plan for addressing Tony's needs, his parents were surprised to be told that the occupational therapist had tested for more than oral-motor issues, and that this therapist had come to the conclusion that Tony was likely autistic. His jumping around was viewed as a red-flag for autism, and it was suggested that he would benefit from wearing a spandex body suit under his cloth-ing to try and stop this. The occupational therapist, the speech-language pathologist, and the early childhood consultant who had become involved all agreed that the best course of action would be to send Tony to the Greenwood Early Intervention School for his pre-school years. This school specialized in behaviourist-style early education.

His parents disagreed. The jumping, they said, was simply the behaviour of an excitable 3-year-old and nothing more. They scoffed at the suggestion of autism, and told the occupational therapist that the body suit suggestion was absurd and that they would not comply. Besides that, they wondered why anything other than oral-motor issues had been examined at all. They disagreed with both therapists that Tony was as severe as they said (this was not their experience at home), and they especially disagreed with the idea of sending him to the Greenwood Early Intervention School. On investigation, his parents discovered that children who attended Greenwood rarely graduated to inclusive school settings. They argued that he was happy in his current day care, had plenty of friends to interact with, and that any therapy could be implemented there or at home. The therapists strongly disagreed and outlined the potential dangers of not following their advice, but on his parents' insistence it was decided that Tony would receive daily speech-language therapy in his current day care, with weekly home consultation. His parents decided that no additional services would be required from the occupational therapist.

After eight months, Tony was re-tested by the speech-language pathologist using the same standardized tests as previous. This time his receptive language was on the 38th percentile, and his expressive language was on the 69th percentile for children his age. He still had some moderate articulation problems. Staff at the day care reported that Tony made friends easily and was able to keep them. He was popular, active, well behaved, loved arts and crafts, and was in most ways much like other children who attended the centre. On the basis of these tests, which were within normal limits, Tony lost his government funding. His parents were pleased about this, but continued to self-finance some speech-language therapy for an addi-tional year.

On entering school Tony was once again tested for speech-language issues, given his history. He once again tested with normal limits, this time with mild articulation problems, which the therapist put down to some immaturity common at that age. His first year of school was very successful. He performed well socially and academi-cally, loved his teacher and school, and was happy both at home and school. This pattern continued throughout his second year of schooling, with his articulation problem being reduced to a barely noticeable lisp.

Tony's parents wondered what his future might have been had they sent him to the Greenwood Early Intervention Centre in a spandex suit.

- Examine the definition of what it means to respect childhood offered earlier in this chapter. In what ways is the approach taken by the therapists in Tony's story inconsistent with respect for the child?
- Examine Figures 1.1 and 1.2. Is there any evidence of these views of children in Tony's story, particularly with respect to ideas about the competent child?
- Identify who was more focused on Tony's present, and who was more focused on his future in the above case study? What were the positive and negative aspects of each point of view?

Discussion Questions

- Where does childhood begin and end?
- This book focuses on westernized ideas of childhood. Are you aware of other cultural views of childhood? What are they?
- Locate and read the United Nations International Convention on the Rights of the Child (1989). Has this been fully implemented in your region?
- Consider Koyama et al.'s (2006) study described in the second window on research in this chapter. What does this say about adults' views of children and childhood?

Further Resources

Greenspan, B. (1978). *Children through the ages: A history of childhood.* New York: Barnes & Noble.

Lorenco, O., & Muchado, A. (1996). In defense of Piaget's theory: A reply to 10 common criticisms. *Psychological Review, 103*(1), 143–64.

Rinaldi, C. (2006). *In dialogue with Reggio Emilia.* London: Routledge.

2 Respecting Children's Present and Future

Chapter Outline

Introduction

This chapter examines the relationship between time and childhood and, more specifically, how children's time is viewed, used, and managed by adults. It discusses the sorts of activities children are involved in at home, school, and in society, and the expectations placed on children with regard to their future lives.

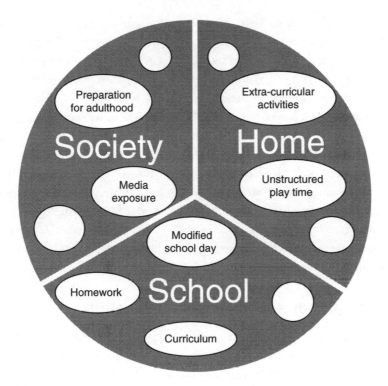

Figure 2.1 Chapter outline figure

The big picture

Childhood as preparation for the future

Few people would agree with the notion that the main purpose of middle-age is to prepare for old-age. More commonly, people might say that middle-age is a time for being productive, for perhaps raising children, and having a satisfying career and family life. Setting aside financial and psychological resources for retirement would be one feature of middle-age, but likely not the defining feature (Hunter & Sundel, 1989). What would define middle-age for most people would be the events that occur during that period, and living in the moment by enjoying those events (King & Hicks, 2007). Erikson (1968, 1980) supported this view of middle-age, saying it is a time when we experience conflict between generativity and stagnation. At this stage of life we try to focus on being productive and avoiding standing still. The value of enjoying each stage of life for what it is, is evident in our views of most other stages of the life cycle. However, many people would agree, either explicitly or through their actions, with the notion that one of the main purposes of childhood is to prepare children to be adults who are happy and well prepared to make a positive contribution to society. Clichés about childhood such as 'children are our future' exist because they reflect what many people believe. Often childhood is not viewed as a stage of life worthy of being experienced on its own terms; it has become a period in life where we tend to view activities largely as preparation for the future (Dahlberg, Moss, & Pence, 1999). However, by focusing too much on preparation for adulthood, we fundamentally disrespect both children's present and future. We require children to devote finite childhood hours to preparing for a future world which we cannot predict, and for which the skills and knowledge learned might not even be relevant. This was recognized well over 100 years ago by John Dewey (1894), however, little seems to have changed since that time with regard to our ideas about children's time.

Perspectives on the purpose of education

That we tend to view childhood as mainly a period of preparation for adulthood is evident in the media and other forms of public discourse. Academics talk about preparing youth, especially those with disabilities, for transition to the adult world (see e.g. Fulligni & Hardaway, 2007). Politicians and business leaders make statements about supporting education and families as a way of ensuring future national economic prosperity. Ben Bernanke (2007), the Chairman of the United States Board of Governors of the Federal Reserve Banking System, remarked in a speech at the US Chamber Education and Workforce Summit that

> I don't really need to convince you that, as an investment, education provides excellent returns, both for individuals and for society. . . . Here I am speaking not just of education acquired formally in classrooms before entering the workforce but also of lifelong learning that, yes, includes the formal classroom training that might first come to mind but that also includes early childhood programs, informal mentoring on the job, and mid-career retraining, to name a few examples. And when I speak of capabilities, I mean not only the knowledge derived from education but also the values, skills, and personal traits acquired through education, which are as important as, and sometimes even more important than, the specific knowledge obtained. (¶2)

In Bernanke's view, educating children is useful because it offers a return for investment in the future. The purpose of education is reduced to the continued production of a useful labour market. Children are reduced to the status of future workers, with their value being equated to what they will one day be capable of producing. While this utilitarian idea of childhood is shared by many, it is not supported by the most influential international agreements pertaining to children. There is little in the internationally recognized United Nations Declaration of the Rights of the Child (1959) or the Convention on the Rights of the Child (1989) to support his future-focused view. Principle 7 of the Declaration states that

> He shall be given an education which will promote his general culture and enable him, on a basis of equal opportunity, to develop his abilities, his individual judgement, and his sense of moral and social responsibility, and to become a useful member of society.

There is nothing in this statement that says that the main focus should be on future outcomes or on producing a viable future workforce. Rather, it states that children should be provided with opportunities to develop and become useful members of society. This does not imply that one should wait until adulthood to see this occur. The purpose of education in this context might be viewed as preparing a child to become a useful member of society in the present; as a child. That children should be viewed as having to somehow perpetuate and even improve future society represents an unfair burden for them (Dahlberg et al., 1999). What a frightening prospect for a young person to have to live with, and be constantly reminded of, that future responsibility.

Even if one were to agree that the purpose of childhood is to prepare children to be successful in the future, how exactly might one go about this? Predicting the future is a dubious prospect at best, and most would concede that it is impossible. Why, then, are some so convinced that they know how to do this? Marcus Aurelius, stoic philosopher and Roman emperor nearly 2000 years ago, brought his perspective to ideas about the future. He said 'Let not future things disturb thee, for thou wilt come to them, if it shall be necessary, having with thee the same reason which thou now usest for present things' (Aurelius, 2006, p. 107). By this Aurelius means that we should live in the present, and be content with developing skills and knowledge which are useful for this present because they will also likely be useful for the future. If we apply this line of thought to childhood in the modern day, then providing children with the skills and knowledge they need to function in society as children in the present, and gradually teaching new skills and knowledge or modifying the old ones as they grow, we are both respecting the present and preparing children adequately for whatever future they may encounter. A successful present in this context results in a successful future, as opposed to more or less ignoring the present as one prepares for the future.

Media encroachments on childhood

The pace at which children are moved towards that future is also problematic. Efforts to encroach on children's present through various means are visible in society through the media. Children are now exposed to sex, violence, and other adult themes more frequently than ever before. In the year 1991, it was estimated that by the age of 16 children had seen over 200,000 violent acts on television (Toomey, 1991). With the increased popularity and availability of graphic video games and the internet (a medium with a reputation for sexual and violent content), it is more than likely that today the impact of such exposures has increased significantly (Feder, Levant, & Dean, 2007). Indeed in the year 2002, more than 90 per cent of the children in the United States played video games, and by the year 2005 an average of 5.5 hours per week for girls, and 13 hours per week for boys were spent playing such games. It has been estimated that as many as 89 per cent of these video games contain some violent content (Carnagey & Anderson, 2005). While some dismiss the role media has in influencing the behaviour of children, there is ample evidence in the research literature that violent images and video games do have a considerable negative impact (Anderson et al., 2003; Carnagey & Anderson, 2005). Krcmar and Hight (2007) found that even a single exposure to action cartoons can cause young children to form mental models for aggression. Exposure to this sort of media content pushes children towards an adult culture of violence. In his analysis of the loss of boyhood on the journey to becoming a man, Groth (2007) observes that

> Video games involving car crashes and medieval jousting and, most recently, 'professional wrestling' melodrama all figure prominently in their fantasies and games and have become part of the collective unconscious of young males. For most, fitting the 'bad boy' image is a prerequisite for attaining manhood. (p. 20)

Children experiencing such adult themes through the media are in essence being robbed of their childhood, entering the adult world earlier than is necessary. Respecting childhood involves limiting access to this content. This is a difficult task considering the extent to which it is infused into everyday life. Laws and regulations directed at protecting children from such media have proven to be only partly effective (Wulff, 2007), the result being that parents and professionals who work with children need to take the responsibility not only to filter out such media from children's lives, but also to educate children to be media safe and stay away from such content when they do encounter it.

Apart from providing a means of exposure to adult themes, the media plays another role in disrespecting the present of childhood by promoting the idea that it is something one should grow out of as quickly as possible. There is an underlying theme in some advertising that it is good to be a big kid, and that to be grown up (and to prove that by purchasing certain products such as toilet training products, clothing, and toys) is desirable. While advertising campaigns which emphasize the positive aspects of growing up serve to perpetuate the notion that childhood should be directed towards the future, they are in essence only responding to wider held views of adults. If these ideas did not resonate with families, and therefore assist in selling products, then they would not feature in advertising. The media is not separate from society. To a large degree it reflects the values and beliefs of the audience it reaches. If adults want to preserve the condition of childhood, then they must look inward and engage in critical self-evaluation of their own values, beliefs, practices, and attitudes with respect to children's time.

Window on Research

Kuntsche (2004) conducted a study of 4,222 Swiss children in Grades 7 and 8 to determine what kind of violence-related behaviour or opinion is directly related to excessive media use among this population. The study found for the total sample significant relationships existed between violence-related media use and each violence-related variable. When broken down into a multivariate comparison, physical violence among boys ceased to be significant. For girls, the playing of violent video games had an impact on the levels of physical violence, however only television viewing was linked to indirect violence for this gender. Kuntsche concludes by saying that 'with the exception of excessive electronic game-playing among girls, this study found that electronic media are not thought to lead directly to real-life violence but to hostility and indirect violence' (p. 230).

Respecting children's present and future at home

Extra-curricular activities and 'hyper-parenting'

Respecting children's present and future is not an issue that is limited only to broader society and school. Children's time also needs to be respected in the home and outside-of-school context. There is considerable debate in the community around the extra-curricular activities which many children participate in outside of school hours. Advocates of such activities point to the health and social benefits, while others question the value in filling children's schedules with organized activities, noting that there is a cost to doing this. On one extreme sit families who ensure that their children lead highly structured and demanding outside-of-school lives, while on the other sit families who provide very little structure (and sometimes even supervision) for their children during these times. Each of these scenarios has implications for respecting children's time, and the literature indicates that that neither of these extremes results in positive outcomes for children.

As regions of the world have become more affluent over the past few decades, there is more leisure time and disposable family income available for many children to participate in a wider range of extra-curricular activities than ever before. The wide range of available extra-curricular activities is evidence of this market demand. Sporting clubs and teams, private tutoring, music lessons, library clubs, church groups, the scout and guide movement, children's hobby clubs, gymnastics, art and craft classes, dance, drama groups, and any number of other activities exist to occupy and perhaps enhance children's lives outside of school hours. These activities have become an accepted part of many cultures, to the point where the term Soccer Mum has become widely recognized. The term conjures up images of a busy mother chauffeuring children around in a van from one extra-curricular activity to another. Some car manufacturers have even capitalized on this, and it has now become an advertising cliché (see e.g. past print and television advertisements for minivans featuring mothers rushing children to various activities, at which soccer balls fall out of opened van doors on arrival). Rosenfeld and Wise (2001) used the term hyper-parenting to describe parents who, with the best of intentions, feel pressure to meet perceived expectations of adults in society to help their children learn and succeed. Trying to keep up with the demands, these families end up living a lifestyle revolving around extracurricular activities. However, while the term has now become part of the popular psychology vernacular (see Honore, 2008, and the numerous internet hyper-parenting websites and chat rooms), the idea is not a new one and has been apparent in scholarly discourse for some time. In the early 1980s, Elkind (1981) was already concerned about the demands being placed on children and families. According to Elkind (2007) these demands have only increased over the decades, resulting in children who have less free and unencumbered time than ever before.

Structuring the spare time of children can begin right from the first few months of life. Classes for very young children, including infants, include anything from gym classes, swimming lessons, and other physical activities, to classes with a more intellectual and cognitive focus such as musical appreciation and Talking Tots in the United Kingdom. Talking Tots provides classes for toddlers which aim to develop social confidence, listening and attention skills, sharing and turn-taking skills, expressive language, word meaning and vocabulary, narrative ability (storytelling), and phonological awareness for reading and writing (Talking Tots, n.d.). Talking Tots is not designed as an early intervention for children with disabilities, but rather as a general educational non-home context in which toddlers can commence formal learning.

Devaluing unstructured play time

The argument that the occasional weekly structured class for toddlers is damaging to them is hard to sustain, and not supported in the available research literature. Indeed, it is likely that in moderation these activities are positive. However, given the plethora of possible choices, it is not surprising that some parents, with all the best intentions, find themselves running from one toddler activity to another on a daily basis. Critics argue that it is not so much the activities in and of themselves that are potentially damaging, but rather that it is the loss of unstructured free play time in order to attend these activities that is troublesome. It has been known for some time that unstructured play is extremely important for child development. Key theorists such as Piaget (1929, 1952), Vygotsky (1978), and Bruner (1966, 1986) have all recognized the value and importance of the role of unstructured play in cognitive development, along with many others before and since. The American Academy of

Pediatrics argued that free play needs to be protected to ensure the 'cognitive, physical, social and emotional well-being of children and youth' (Ginsburg, the AAP Committee on Communications, & the AAP Committee on Psychological Aspects of a Child and Family Health, 2006, p. 1). That there is a problem with protecting this need and right to free play is evident in a letter to the *London Daily Telegraph* newspaper signed by 270 recognized scholars and child development professionals from the United Kingdom and around the world. Concern was expressed over 'the marked decline over the last 15 years in children's play. Play – particularly outdoor, unstructured, loosely supervised play – appears to be vital to children's all-round health and well-being' (Barlow et al., 2007, ¶3). Attending enjoyable classes and groups with very young children can be a rewarding pastime for both parent and child. However, there is a need to remain cognisant and respectful of the need for large amounts of unstructured play time, especially for very young children. This is one way of respecting the present of these children.

Once children reach school age the issue of respecting unstructured time becomes more acute, as for the majority of the day these children attend very structured school settings. They may then be involved in structured after-school sporting or other activities. Once again, these activities are often enjoyable for children, and if done in moderation are beneficial. Indeed, research has supported some positive aspects of such pursuits (see Gilman, Meyers, & Perez, 2004; Mahoney, 2000). Depending on the circumstances, these can include a reduction in some forms of substance abuse, higher grades and academic aspirations, and more positive attitudes towards school in general (Darling, 2005). The concern, however, that school-age children are over-programmed outside of school hours is not easily dismissed. Further, the benefits of out-of-school activities are not as far-reaching as might be deduced from the existing research. For example, extra-curricular activities have not been found to result in the reduction of all types of substance abuse (alcohol use, one of the most common forms of teen substance abuse, has not been found to decrease), or adolescent depression (Darling, 2005). Those who support the view that children are over-programmed cite similar evidence in support of their arguments as those who advocate for extra-curricular activities. For example, Gilbert (1999) speaks of the 'after-school pressure cooker', noting that children are increasingly becoming exhausted due to over scheduling, and that

> The pressure is the greatest when they are shuttled not to activities that they want to do, but to activities that their parents want them to do. Doctors say that

some children feel so much pressure for high performance that they develop stress-related symptoms like insomnia, stomachaches, headaches, anxiety, and depression. (p. F7)

Despite some evidence that extra-curricular activities have become a scapegoat for many of the pressures placed on children (Luthar, Shoum, & Brown, 2006), there is clearly some merit to the argument that children are at times overburdened with extra-curricular activities. Some child specialists in widely circulated popular magazines have advocated encouraging children to participate in structured activities even if they are reluctant. Hartley-Brewer (2006), in her discussion of the benefits of extra-curricular activities, advises that 'If your child, for now, is happier at home, try inviting friends over, encourage lots of interests, and give him a bigger role in deciding what to do until he's more confident' (p. 67). By being more confident Hartley-Brewer means more willing to participate in structured activities outside of school hours, rather than informal play at home. The United Nations Convention on the Rights of the Child (1989), however, recognizes 'the right of the child to rest and leisure, to engage in play and recreational activities appropriate to the age of the child and to participate freely in cultural life and the arts' (article 31). It is clear from this that all children are entitled to time for play as well as recreation. Given that two terms are mentioned, a distinction might be made between the two. Spontaneous games devised during free time with friends or alone might be considered play, while structured activities such as those cited above might be considered as recreation. Mahoney et al. (2007) note that over the past two decades children have lost 12 hours of free time a week, including 8 hours of unstructured play time, and that the majority of this time has been lost to structured extra-curricular activities. In order to respect the intent of the United Nations Convention on the Rights of the Child (1989), consideration should be given to the reclamation of this free time to strike greater balance.

Being respectful of children's present at home, then, involves creating a balance between structured activities outside of school hours, and time for free, unstructured play in environments which are supported by the adults in their lives. This approach has support in the literature with regard to physical, cognitive, and psychological development (Ginsburg et al., 2006) and, frankly, is just good common sense. What exactly is the right balance is context dependent, however, if the adults in a child's life find their schedules exhausting and demanding, they can be fairly certain that the children are feeling much the same way.

Window on Research

Cosden, Morrison, Gutierrez, and Brown (2004) examined how children spend their time after school and how activities, including homework, can contribute to school success. They conducted a literature review that specifically focused on after-school academic assistance programmes, namely the Gervitz Homework Project, after-school activities and school achievement, and parental involvement. They concluded that after-school homework programmes provide some children with the structure they need and improve academic success at school, however they also have the potential to interfere with family and community activities.

Respecting children's present and future at school

Schools can impact children's time in three significant ways. First, the structure and organization of the school day has direct bearing on how children are able to experience the present while attending school. Secondly, school places expectations and demands on children's time beyond the boundaries of the school day through assigning homework and assignments which must be completed outside of formal class time. Finally, the curriculum in which children are engaged in while at school impacts both their present and future lives.

Squeezing the school day

Until recently the traditional structure of the school day has, by and large, changed very little, with formal classes usually being interspersed with a couple of short breaks, and a longer one for lunch. Some schools, however, have now started to change the duration and structure of breaks. This might have occurred in part as the result of pressures from an ever-expanding curriculum, or as the result of pedagogical ideas calling for longer class periods which can assist students to engage in more meaningful learning events (Griggs & Griggs, 1993). Regardless of the rationale behind this shift, the end result in some places where this has been implemented has been a loss of time for free play (Austin, 1998). Some have viewed the loss of unstructured play time at school as an infringement on the basic human rights of children. Dubroc (2007) argues that the recent trend of eliminating school recess time in favour of longer instructional blocks at school is in violation of the 1989 Convention on the Rights of the Child because this is a time when children should be permitted to rest and engage in free play during the school day. The results of her content-analysis study suggest that 'For school age children, breaks are essential not only to healthy cognitive development, but to reduce or eliminate stress and the promotion of a sedentary lifestyle, which can lead to depression, obesity, suicide or overall poor mental health' (p. 2).

The loss of break times, however, is just one element of structured school days which fail to respect the unique features of childhood. School days tend to be built around set times for the beginning and ending of classes or school activities. While the benefits of this approach are that it offers predictability and routine to children, the disadvantage is that learning can become compartmentalized and not be seen as something which should necessarily be connected to other parts of a child's life, or which can be adjusted according to the needs of children. In response to this some schools have made adjustments to their schedules to allow greater blocks of instructional time for children to engage in cross-curricular learning (Griggs & Griggs, 1993).

The Time, Learning, and Afterschool Task Force (2007) suggests that the traditional structure of the school day is now obsolete. They advocate school day structures that have greater continuity with children's lives outside of school. This is based on a recognition that learning can occur at all times in a child's day, and need not always be addressed in what they consider to be contrived educational circumstances at school. The Time, Learning, and Afterschool Taskforce vision is that

> We see communities of policymakers, institutions, and individuals, working together to make sure that all students have optimum opportunities to learn and grow into responsible citizens. Up to now, policy making around how children use their learning time has been mostly school-based. Yet, the majority of time available for learning occurs outside of the traditional school day. (p. 13)

While the sentiment that schools need to examine how the structure of their days meets the needs of children is consistent with adopting a more respectful use of their time, the broader vision of the Time, Learning, and Afterschool Taskforce is perhaps something that should be considered with care. The report concludes with the words 'In a new day for learning there is no final bell' (p. 47). The idea that time for learning essentially never finishes might be true in a technical sense (we are, after all, always learning), however it does raise the spectre of children never being able to escape being taught in their lives outside of school, once again putting pressure on the availability of free time to play. While it is important that schools adjust to meet the needs of children, ideas which might end up placing further restrictions on children's free time should give pause, even where they are connected to producing more sensitive and flexible school environments. Consideration needs to be given to the notion that there are times in children's lives when they are entitled to downtime, to simply engage in play, rest, or other activities purely for enjoyment and their aesthetic qualities. This is especially important in light of calls from some sectors of society to lengthen the school day and even the school year through a reduction in holiday time so as to allow greater time for formal learning (Hambrook et al., 2007). Children are already under time pressures both at school and at home (Honore, 2008), and further adding to this pressure by lengthening formal learning time, or by extending it into the after-school environment, is clearly adult-driven rather than pedagogically justified. While there is some anecdotal support in the literature for a lengthened school day (Farbman, 2007), there is little empirical research evidence to support the effectiveness of this approach. While a number of schools in Massachusetts in the United States have moved to a longer school day, at this point there is no objective data to support the success or otherwise of their approach, or the possible negative side effects resulting from more time in school.

Opting out of time tyranny

Adjusting the structure of the school day in order to make it more meaningful and appropriate for children is complex. The answer likely lies not in extending the school day or year, or in reducing children's opportunities for free play, but rather in innovative, flexible, and more fluid scheduling within schools. It seems a relatively simple task on the surface, however any moves to produce more responsive school schedules will likely be confounded by issues of space, industrial workplace agreements and employment contracts, transport to and from schools, community expectations, and a traditional educational culture of teachers working in discrete blocks within discrete subject boundaries. There is no simple solution, and each school and educational jurisdiction would need to engage in radical and likely uncomfortable reform in order to change the existing structures. It is, however, reform worth undertaking. Dahlberg et al. (1999) provide some thoughts on practice in Reggio Emilia with respect to the structure of time in an educational institution. They point out that one aspect of the pedagogical work in this system is

> a refusal to be time governed. Most children attend early childhood institutions for at least a full school day, and at least for three years, often longer. Time is not organized by the clock, but according to children's own sense of time, their personal rhythms and what they need for the projects on which they are working. All this gives children time to get engaged, not to have to hurry, time to do things with satisfaction. (p. 60)

While the system in Reggio relates to early childhood education, the ideas and philosophy behind this time-structure have implications for educational contexts for children beyond this age, and so are worth consideration.

Homework: Valuable learning opportunity or meaningless waste of time?

While lengthening the school day is, with the exception of some isolated cases, still an academic argument, schools have in reality always reached beyond that boundary. Homework has been a feature of the school experience for generations, and continues to be to this day. Those who advocate assigning homework point to the contribution it makes to academic success at school (Cosden et al., 2004; Heitzmann, 2007). Simplicio (2005) calls it 'a time honored strategy for developing learning skills and reinforcing knowledge gained in the classroom' (p. 138). He further notes that 'study after study show that homework, from the elementary through the university level, is an effective method for reinforcing educational learning goals' (p. 138), although he does not specifically cite which studies those are.

There are some, however, who question the value of homework altogether, both in terms of its efficacy as a mechanism for learning, and also because of the impact it has on family time. Kohn (2006a) suggests that research relating to activities which occur outside of school hours, and specifically homework, has been abused and that such research might be considered dysfunctional, or at the very least drastically and perhaps deliberately misinterpreted. Kohn (2006a, 2006b, 2007a, 2007b) argues that there is virtually no support for the efficacy of homework to be found in the research literature (if it is critically examined) and that it is detrimental to children's schedules, family relationships, and personal lives. Stager (2006) supports

Kohn's views, arguing that 'few of the justifications for homework pass the giggle test' (p. 74). According to Stager, homework has a negative impact on family relationships and is a form of family surveillance being undertaken by schools in order to ensure that children are always in some way connected to school, even when they are not physically on campus. A recent large Canadian study (N = 5,361) found that 72 per cent of parents with children aged 5–24 cited homework as a source of family stress. Canadian adolescents do an average of 9.2 hours of homework per week, making it the second-most time-consuming adolescent activity in Canada. Despite this, Canadians have seemingly become so accustomed to homework that they do not even question its value despite the stress it causes, as 80 per cent of those surveyed also agreed that it develops good work habits and enhances learning (Canadian Council on Learning, 2007).

Even very young children can have homework expectations placed on them. It is common for teachers of children in the early years of school to use home reading programmes which require children to engage in daily reading. Indeed, some reading programmes are likely positive in that they encourage family participation and provide an opportunity for bonding (Stratton-Lemieux, 2007). Home reading is a fairly low-key approach to homework, and it is hard to sustain an argument that asking children to read for a short period each day is unreasonable, providing there are no consequences for those times when children miss a day or two of home reading because of other events in their lives. Indeed, reading should be encouraged because it can enrich children's lives and expand their intellectual horizons. What should be of concern is the assigning of more traditional forms of homework to very young children. Seo and Bruk (2003) describe a structured mathematics homework programme for very young children attending an Early Childhood Centre involving hands-on activities. The teachers in this study 'considered homework to be an effective tool for familiarizing parents with the kinds of hands-on mathematics taught at school and helping parents promote their children's mathematical learning both in and out of the context of the homework' (p. 27). Although Seo and Bruk show an awareness of the possible inappropriateness of such a programme, it is presented in highly positive terms because the children are seen as enjoying the extra work and the parents are interested in it. Based on this, homework for pre-school children is accepted and assigned value. Similarly, Bailey (2006) presents the results of her research on reading, and argues that carefully designed homework can be helpful in improving parent–child interactions and learning outcomes for at-risk young children. Bailey's study examined homework with reference to a relatively low-key home reading programme similar to those discussed above. In practice, this was likely positive and placed little demands on free time, however, what is striking, but not surprising given the widespread acceptance of homework, is that the legitimacy of homework in and of itself is not questioned in the study, rather, it is seen as an accepted part of life for children in Grade 2. Instead of arguing that young children's lives will be better if homework delivery is improved, consideration should be given to alternative ways of improving parent–child interactions and academic performance which do not involve schools imposing themselves on families. Rather than young children and their families spending time working on tasks essentially designed and assigned by schools, perhaps providing more time and support for families to engage in enjoyable activities in the community would be a brighter and more productive way of eliciting the same outcomes. This approach would respect children's time outside of school, and would also recognize and value the importance of family life.

It is clear that homework is a contentious issue, and even those who support it concede that the ways in which it is generally assigned by teachers results in little benefit for children. Simplicio's (2005) solution to the problem is to recognize that teachers will never stop assigning homework, and that it will always be a part of an overburdened schedule. He suggests that time at the end of the school day should be set aside for children to complete their homework under teacher supervision. This suggestion effectively amounts to extending the school day, which in terms of respecting children's time, as discussed above, is an inadequate response. Indeed, while most supporters of homework recognize that it has been poorly implemented, none are able to produce viable alternatives which adequately respect the child (Cosden et al., 2004; Heitzmann, 2007). Most often they amount to minor tinkering with an already ineffectual strategy. What, then, is the solution? Simplicio's (2005) suggestion that teachers will never stop assigning homework will certainly be the case as long as the idea that it is valuable and required is perpetuated. Some schools, however, have now implemented policies regarding the non-assignment of homework (Leonie, 2005; Stager, 2006) and teachers themselves have sometimes cooperated in formulating such policies. Abolishing homework is not the radical idea it may seem, and may have value for both children and teachers in terms of time, angst in getting it completed, and overall respect for children's lives outside of school hours. In the words of Kohn (2007a) 'Daily homework is the rule in most schools. Why not make it the exception?' (p. 1).

Future-focused curriculum

While school can impact children's time in a negative way as a result of school structures and outside of school hours expectations, school curriculum is a further area in which children's present and future are often simultaneously disrespected. What children learn while they are at school is often focused solely on the future with little thought to the present. Indeed, if anything relevant to the present is learned, it is often incidental to the larger focus of producing adults who have relevant skills and knowledge. For example, while there is a reference to success while at school, the aims of the United Kingdom National Curriculum are clearly focused on the future.

> Education influences and reflects the values of society, and the kind of society we want to be. It is important, therefore, to recognize a broad set of common purposes, values and aims that underpin the school curriculum and the work of schools. Clear aims that focus on the qualities and skills learners need to succeed in school and beyond should be the starting point for the curriculum. (Qualifications and Curriculum Authority, n.d., ¶1)

Indeed, one of the two purposes of the UK National Curriculum relates solely to the future. The curriculum 'prepares learners at the school for the opportunities, responsibilities and experiences of adult life' (¶2). This is not uncommon or surprising. Statements such as this exist in curriculum documents all over the world, including Australia, Canada, the United States, and throughout Europe and other regions and nations. According to the UK Qualifications and Curriculum Authority (n.d.)

> To be well equipped for their future, young people need to develop essential skills for learning, life and employment. As well as the skills that relate to learning in specific subjects, there are other more generic skills essential to life and work. There is widespread consensus that skills such as self-management, problem solving, teamwork and effective communication are important components in a curriculum that seeks to prepare young people for the future. ('skills' ¶1)

Perhaps this situation needs to be reconsidered in light of a respectful view of children's present. In Alberta, Canada, in 2005, then Minister of Education Lyle Oberg required all schools to implement 30 minutes per day of physical activity for all children in Grades 1–9. Schools had difficulty accommodating this extra requirement for a number of reasons, however the idea behind it provides an example of curriculum possibilities which respect both children's present and future. The requirement was made in response to rising childhood obesity levels across Canada. The additional 30 minutes of physical education was implemented in an attempt to assist children in reducing obesity levels both in the present, and also to promote more active and healthy lifestyles in the future as they learned to incorporate exercise into their daily routines. This requirement, regardless of the way in which it was devised and implemented, supported children's needs in both the present and future.

In order to respect children's present and future while they are in school, what they learn in terms of curriculum should be of benefit to them as children living in the present first and foremost. Considerations as to what sorts of skills and knowledge they will need for the distant future are important, but should work in concert with what children need in the present. The future is unpredictable, therefore the skills and knowledge children will need for that future are equally unpredictable. Of course, no responsible education system and curriculum can afford to ignore the future, but it needs to be recognized that most of what children need to learn in order to be successful children in the present will also be relevant in the future. These include social skills, problem solving abilities, literacy in all its forms, knowledge and positive attitudes about health and fitness, self-confidence, and the capacity to be flexible and engage in life-long learning, among others. Curriculum which ignores this in favour of teaching rudimentary knowledge and skills for the future fundamentally disrespects children.

Window on Research

Cheung and Leung Ngai (1992) conducted survey research involving 1,983 children in Grades 3–6 in 53 randomly selected Hong Kong schools. The study examined stressors related to homework, with the self-administered questionnaire also asking about homework completion time and any somatic, anxiety, and depression symptoms which were manifested as the result of homework. Four components were associated with the stressors including time required to complete daily homework, workload of homework, difficulty and monotony of homework, and social pressures placed on the children to complete homework.

They found that the median time required to complete daily homework in Hong Kong was 1.5 to 2 hours. A number of gender differences were identified in various areas, including completion time (which was higher for girls) and levels of social pressure (which were greater for boys). The most important finding of this study was a correlation between social pressure and content and workload of homework, and somatic, anxiety, and depression symptoms including headaches, faintness, loss of appetite, stomach aches, self-derogation, crying, suicidal thoughts, insomnia, and bad dreams.

Cheung and Leung Ngai (1992) suggested that educators need to closely monitor the amount and content of the homework they assign, and be aware of the pressures which exist in students lives related to homework.

Case Study: Education in Taiwan – Going to Extremes

Taiwan has been associated with high levels of student academic achievement on some international measures (Martin, Gonzalez, & Chrostowski, 2004), however the negative effect the education system has had on individual children and the collective experience of childhood in that country deserves scrutiny. Kao (2001) examined Taiwanese children's stress resulting from the often intense after-school lives of these children. While Kao's study found that these children tended to suffer from a somewhat elevated risk of stress if they were involved in after-school activities that they did not consider to be enjoyable, the larger issue addressed by the study, the reason for its being conducted in the first place, was the considerable amount of time spent by many Taiwanese children in outside-of-school activities which are often academic in focus. Consider the following experience of a foreign teacher working in Taiwan:

'I was working in a "cram" English Language school which was open from 4:00 p.m. to 9.30 p.m. most days of the week, Saturdays from 7:00 a.m. until 9.30 p.m., and Sundays beginning in the afternoon. Classes would last from between 90 minutes and 120 minutes with a 10-minute break, and children would generally attend twice a week. On other days they would attend other "cram" schools which taught math, science, and other curriculum areas. Some students literally attended school for excessively long days 7 days a week. It was not uncommon for even very young children of 5 years old to attend extra classes for music, languages or school curriculum areas from 7:00 a.m., go to school following that until 3.30 p.m., then attend after-school classes until 9.30 p.m. I even tutored a 7-year-old girl after this series of classes, in a session which began at 10:00 p.m. I worked for a time at a non-government approved but not uncommon English language kindergarten (because young children were not permitted to learn English) with children of 2 years old who were expected to sit in chairs facing the front of the classroom for periods in excess of 30 minutes at a time. These children would then go directly to a second 30-minute class. Once a week older students would write journals which were almost entirely focused on ever-present upcoming tests, and feelings of stress anticipating these tests, especially the big test which they needed to do well on to get into a good High School. These children lived a life entirely focused on study, and from what I could see the older a Taiwanese student got, the more they assumed an unhappy and almost despondent posture. You would see them walking with shoulders slumped and heads down, like they were being constantly oppressed' (Name withheld, personal communication, 15 October 2007).

- Considering the *International Declaration of the Rights of the Child*, what concern might there be with these educational practices in Taiwan?
- Are there any correlations between the practices described in this case study and practices in other regions of the world, including your own?
- What are the positive and negative aspects of the Taiwanese approach?

This chapter has examined the issue of time, and how adults intrude and place expectations on children with respect to the use of their time, both present and future. Children's time is fundamentally viewed as needing to be used productively to prepare them for the world of the future. In order to produce the sorts of adults needed for the future, children are expected to sacrifice the present by leading lives of activity and learning, in which time is best spent engaged in schoolwork or other activities judged by adults as being worthwhile. This chapter argues that while engagement with school and other structured activities can be beneficial for children, care needs to be taken to ensure that adequate time is allowed for children to play and rest freely, and to engage in activities relevant to their immediate lives.

Discussion Questions

- To what extent are children you know involved in extra-curricular activities? What is a healthy level of extra-curricular activity?
- What are your views on homework? Why? Why do teachers assign it?
- What positive examples have you seen in the media of children using their spare time?
- How does curriculum impact children's time?

Further Resources

Emmett, J., & Harry, R. (2003). *Ruby in her own time*. New York: Scholastic.

Heitzmann, R. (2007). Target homework to maximize learning. *Education Digest*. March issue.

Kohn, A. (2006). *The homework myth: Why our kids get too much of a bad thing*. USA: Da Capo Books.

United Nations Declaration of the Rights of the Child. Located at www.unhchr.ch/html/menu3/b/25.htm

3 Respecting Children's Relationships and Family Life

Introduction

This chapter examines children's relationships with those closest to them – usually their families – as well as with others in broader social networks of friends, professionals, community members, and others who children typically come into contact with in the course of their lives. Some of the societal conditions that have had an impact on the nature and quality of these relationships are discussed.

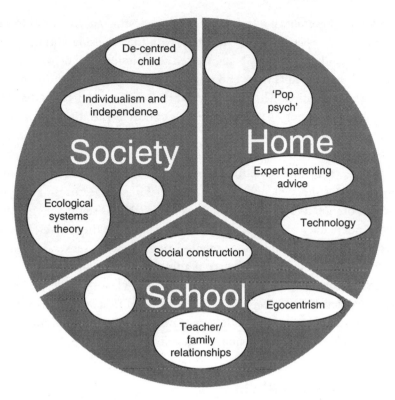

Figure 3.1 Chapter outline figure

The big picture

The independent child

The previous chapter examined the notion of adult imposition on children's time, often in an attempt to try and better prepare them for the future. A common feature of this notion of preparation is the promotion of independence in children so as to allow them to become adults who can be self-sufficient and productive, able to rely on their own resources in order to support themselves. This individualistic view of childhood has developed in concert with western cultural changes over the past few hundred years. Scull (1977), in his examination of how people with mental illness became institutionalized, observes that with the advent of capitalism feudal communities began to break down. Members of those communities began to be seen in terms of their individual capacity to produce profit. This, among many other factors from the Enlightenment through to the present day, contributed to a growing emphasis of a notion of individualism, which is now widely evident throughout society. This emphasis on individual power and control over one's own destiny has led adults to value the importance of personal independence, with the opposing notion of being dependant on others generally being viewed as undesirable (Fineman, 2004).

The notion that adults value and promote independence in children barely requires substantiation. The field of disability studies, especially, has at its core notions of promoting independence in children with disabilities (Baker, Brightman, & Blacher, 2004). Outside of the disability arena, the promotion of independence is also viewed as an essential element in the upbringing of all children. Truby (2007) outlines ways in which to organize classrooms to promote greater independence. Prior to describing the features of a specific classroom designed to do this, she quotes the teacher as saying 'It's all meant to foster independence . . . the more students can do for themselves, I feel I've succeeded' (p. 26). Outside of the school setting, Trost, Biesecker, Stattin, and Kerr (2007) conducted a study to see if adolescents who were reducing their involvement with their parents were demonstrating healthy independence or signs of problems. The acceptance in this study of independence as being a healthy alternative to stronger adolescent relationships with parents reflects the widely held belief that autonomy is desirable.

The interdependent child

The notion of independence, however, needs to be questioned, especially in light of its impact on children's relationships and family life. Bronfenbrenner's (1979) Ecological Systems Theory conceptualizes children as existing within five systems: the microsystem, mesosystem, exosystem, macrosystem, and chronosystem (Figure 3.2). The microsystem comprises individuals and contexts in immediate proximity to the child such as family, peers, and school. The fact that these individuals and contexts exist within a system implies interaction and relationships between the child and the other protagonists. This feature of relationship is central to Bronfenbrenner's theory, and applies not only to the microsystem, but equally also to the other systems he identified. The mesosystem extends further from the child to include the relationships between a child's immediate environments, for example between schools and the home environment, or the neighbourhood peer group and the home. Bronfenbrenner described the mesosystem as 'a system of microsystems. It is formed or extended whenever the developing person moves into a new setting' (p. 25). The exosystem extends to environments which might not directly impact a child's experience, but which are influential nonetheless because

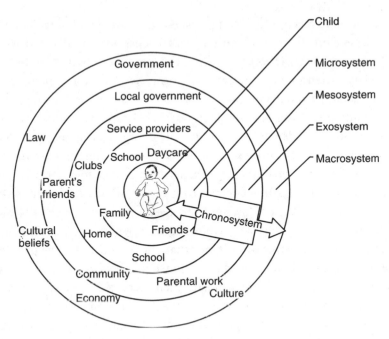

Figure 3.2 Visual model of Bronfenbrenner's (1979) Ecological Systems Theory

they impact people around them. For example, a parent's place of employment does not usually directly impact a child, but if that parent were required to work varied shifts and was often tired during the day, the workplace could be said to indirectly impact the parent–child relationship. Bronfenbrenner also cited sibling's classrooms, the local school board, and the parent's network of friends as belonging to the exosystem because they can all impact the child, even though the child is not an active participant in these environments. The macrosystem relates to society and the larger cultural context in which a child lives. It refers to subcultures and whole cultures 'along with any belief systems or ideology underlying such constituencies' (p. 26). The chronosystem relates to patterns and experiences that tend to occur and reoccur over the lifespan. Although the child sits at the centre of Bronfenbrenner's model (it is more or less child-centred, especially at the microsystem level), if we accept it we must also accept that people are never truly independent, and that raising children with a strong sense of needing to be independent might be doing them a disservice. What is central to Bronfenbrenner's work is the notion of relationship, of interconnectedness and interdependence, rather than independence.

The notion of raising children to exist within the context of relationships, and to depend on others, has been a topic of discussion in academic discourse for some time. Dewey (1894) recognized the interconnectedness of the child and society. According to Dewey 'he is stimulated to act as a member of a unity, to emerge from his original narrowness of action and feeling, and to conceive of himself from the standpoint of the welfare of the group to which he belongs' (p. 77). Independence should not be completely ignored, of course. It is important to be able to do some things for yourself. Further, if a person is going to be interdependent then he/she needs to be able to contribute something of value to the relationship and so must know how to do some things for themselves and others. This, however, speaks more to competency rather than independence. It is possible to be competent without being independent (Leeds, 2005), and it is this competency that one should seek to help children make positive contributions to the relationships they are in. If one accepts that people are never fully independent, then increased emphasis on raising children who have the ability to function as a part of an interdependent social system is needed. Leeds (2005) provides a cogent argument for the promotion of greater interdependence in children. He argues that most of what is done in and outside of school involves interdependence, from teacher–student and student–student interactions, right down to acknowledging the use of the ideas of others through appropriate citation of sources in school assignments. He calls for reform which recognizes and supports the value of this interdependence. According to Leeds 'learning the types of imagination and empathy suitable for all types of social interactions should be a central goal of education' (p. 54).

The decentred child: A postmodern view

Rinaldi (2006) and Dahlberg et al. (1999) advance the notion of the decentred child. According to Dahlberg et al. modernism has constructed children as developing a single, rigid identity in which they sit at the centre as 'a static and essentialized self' (p. 57). The postmodern idea of the decentred child views identities being constructed in more fluid, multiple ways, grounded in relationship. According to Dahlberg et al.

> Postmodern conditions bring processes of individualization. But they also foreground relationships. Knowledge, identity, and culture are constituted in relation to others – they are co-constructed. Relational concepts abound: dialogue, conversation, negotiation, encounter, confrontation, conflict . . . a child

is connected to many different groups of shifting ethnic, religious, cultural, and social character. (p. 58)

Children, then, can be viewed in terms of their wider relationships with the sorts of ecological systems identified by Bronfenbrenner (1979) above. The difference here, however, is that Bronfenbrenner placed the child at the centre of the microsystem (although it could be argued that the interrelated nature of the mesosystem is to an extent a precursor of the decentred child). The decentred child has been shifted (see Figure 3.3) with the result that relationships take on a higher level of significance than previous. Given this, the notion of promoting independence needs to be reconsidered in terms of what is most respectful to the state of childhood.

Valuing a child's relationships, and acknowledging the importance of interconnectedness and relationships that occur in the context of a child's daily life, while at the same time promoting individual competence, represents an appropriate and respectful way of living and working with children in society. In practice this raises the idea that perhaps a narrow focus on the individual does children a disservice, and that in order to properly support and respect children one needs to support the ecosystems, the contexts, in which they live.

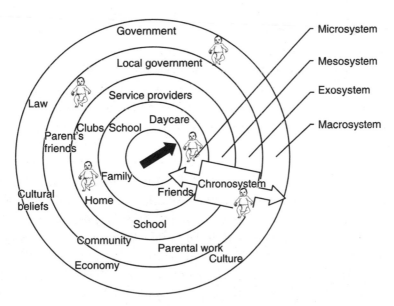

Figure 3.3 Reconciling the decentred child with Bronfenbrenner's (1979) Ecological Systems Theory

Window on Research

Wang (2007) investigated the long-term contribution of maternal elaborative reminiscing to children's development of autobiographical memory ability in a cross-cultural context. Using interviews with pre-school age children and mothers in China, Chinese immigrant families, and non-Chinese families in the United States, Wang collected data at three points in the life of the children, when they were 3 years old (N = 189 mother–child pairs), 3.5 years old (N = 170 mother–child pairs), and 4.5 years old (N = 153 mother–child pairs). The study found that at each age the Euro-American mothers used a more elaborative style than the mothers of both Chinese groups (meaning the Euro-American mothers offered more information on each topic addressed), and Euro-American children could describe more memories than their Chinese peers. The Euro-American elaborative reminiscing was positively associated with mothers' value orientation towards independence (relative to interdependence). According to Wang, this 'reflects the underlying value of constructing elaborate personal narratives and, in turn, a unique individual identity in Euro-American culture' (p. 468).

Respecting children's relationships and family life at home

The most immediate of Bronfenbrenner's (1979) ecological systems discussed above – the microsystem – most commonly exists in the context of a child's family life. Children's first and primary relationship with others is generally with the parents, siblings, and other family members which children commonly see on a daily, or almost daily, basis. The idea of the traditional nuclear family, with two parents of opposite gender and children, has become an increasingly inadequate way of looking at what constitutes a family. Some nations have now defined families as including same-sex partners, single parents, extended relatives and caregivers other than the parents, and adoptive and foster parents. According to UNESCO (1995) 'Families assume diverse forms and functions from one country to another and are a reflection of the pluralism that enriches the world community' (p. 1). Further, the United Nations Convention on the Rights of the Child (1989) recognizes the importance of the family as the fundamental unit which exists to support the care and well-being of children. Regardless of how one defines what constitutes a family, they are important groupings of people that serve functions both for society, and for all members of the family group, including children. At the heart of the family sits the notion of relationship, interconnectedness, and interdependence between the various members (Bornstein, 2005). If children exist through their relationships, if they are part of a series of ecological systems, then to interfere with these relationships represents a disregard for the child. Unfortunately, there are now many external factors which interfere with children's relationships with other members of the family.

The negative impact of popular psychology

Adult members of the family, usually the parents, can become victims of probably well-intentioned but nonetheless bad advice in the form of expert commentary in the media and some popular psychology texts aimed at parents. This advice can often have a significant detrimental impact on family relationships. That adults tend to value expertise is evident. The news media tends to seek out expert opinion related to breaking news items. Governments and businesses consult experts to aid their decision making (Turner, 2001). Most individuals at some time or the other seek the advice of experts, whether it is accountants at tax time, doctors when illness strikes, or lawyers when making significant decisions such as writing wills. Turner (2001), citing Foucault and Derrida, argues that while many claims to expertise fail to gain acceptance, those that do are fraught with issues of power and legitimacy.

Most bookstores now contain shelves of books on parenting advice and any other number of popular psychology topics related to children and child development. Parents, influenced by a culture which says that experts should be listened to, and feeling insecure about their own levels of expertise, read and sometimes act on the advice of these books. According to Bornstein (2005) 'parents today are less secure in their roles, even in the face of environmental and institutional demands that they assume increasing responsibility for their offspring' (p. 311). Many of these books have value and can offer helpful suggestions to parents willing to pick and choose what they learn and use. However, it is also true that some books in that market either contain ideas which themselves are disrespectful towards children and family relationships, or alternatively are so difficult to implement that parents inevitably fail at doing what the book says and end up feeling worse than ever. This is the case with some of the more popular books of advice for parents.

For example, Maggie Mamen's (2006) *The pampered child syndrome: How to recognize it, how to manage it, and how to avoid it*, argues that parents have produced children who are 'loved too much' and who, having had all their needs met throughout their lives, have turned into spoiled brats as a result.

While highly popular, this book and others like it simply pander to popular and almost entirely unsubstantiated negative notions about children. Despite some tepid protestations to the contrary, Mamen places the blame for producing such children mainly on their parents. This is evident in many of the reasons she gives for how her syndrome has come about. She describes the topic in quasi-clinical terms as a 'syndrome' (albeit with a sort of disclaimer regarding this on the back cover), while at the same time offering no meaningful empirical evidence to support the contention that such a phenomenon even exists.

Michelle Borba's (2004) *Don't give me that attitude!: 24 rude, selfish, insensitive things kids do and how to stop them*, focuses on themes similar to Mamen, taking the line that children are assuming a variety of negative roles and behaviours as a result of their upbringing. Borba provides numerous lists and checklists for diagnosing and remedying the 24 negative behaviours she addresses. As with Mamen, parents often bear the brunt of the blame. Simplistic, obvious procedures in the form of lock-step checklists for fixing the problems described in the book are provided. This book, like Mamen's and others by Borba, implicitly advocates authoritarian, top-down behaviour on the part of parents, even though research has shown for some time that this style of parenting can have a negative impact on children (see Patterson, DeBaryshe, & Ramsey, 1989; Pettit, Harrist, Bates, & Dodge, 1991). Further, the general tone of the advice does not take context into account. There is little recognition that children are complex and diverse, as are the situations in which they live.

At the other end of the spectrum is advice from those who believe that an appropriate relationship with a child is one in which the child has all needs, or perceived needs, met immediately and constantly. Although advice such as this generally comes from an underlying philosophy of nurturing and kindness, it can also have a negative impact on a child's relationships with other family members. For example, Sears and Sears (2002, 2005) recommend parents engage in what is known as attachment parenting, especially parents of babies who are fussy. Although their ideas are considerably better supported in research than Mamen and Borba above, they are not always practical. They suggest that parents literally wear their babies in a sling as much as possible. These slings provide a hands-free way for parents to go about their daily lives while wearing the baby. Attachment parenting involves, wherever possible, anticipating and meeting virtually all the needs of a baby, sleeping with the baby, and engaging in marathon nursing sessions if a baby likes to feed frequently and for long periods of time. According to

Sears and Sears (2002) in *The fussy baby: How to bring out the best in your high-need child*, 'babies are takers and mothers are givers' (p. 121). The term attachment parenting is a loaded one. Few parents want to experience the opposite condition – alienation – but the demands placed on parents to constantly be tethered to their baby, breastfeeding at will, and sacrificing even their own bed is unreasonable for many people. Those who cannot keep up with these demands may feel guilty, as if they are not willing to make the necessary sacrifices for their baby and are therefore lesser parents. Those who can keep up must be awfully tired. The necessity of the inclusion of a chapter late in *The fussy baby* on 'How to avoid burnout' speaks volumes.

Respecting a child's relationships with parents involves more than simply anticipating and meeting every need of the child. It takes at least two to have a relationship, and if the parents are feeling exhausted and under pressure to behave in certain ways, then even though the child might be constantly with the parent in a physical sense, the wider relationship might be under threat. Notwithstanding his infamous inability to follow his own advice, and other problems inherent in his work (Maier, 1998), Spock (1988) suggests an approach which might be more helpful to both parties, and therefore to the relationship. Spock says

> When I suggested in *Baby and child care* that beginning parents with a colicky or fretful baby try to take a couple of nights off a week, together or separately, it was not to encourage irresponsibility but to try to prevent the parents from becoming physically and emotionally exhausted. This sometimes happens (and usually to the mother) when a baby's crying lasts four hours a night for three months and the two parents, tense and distressed, sit and take it. Even in cases in which there is no misery in the baby, I think it's sensible for highly conscientious, first-time parents to take a little time off and keep up with friends and interests, if possible. Otherwise some of them become totally obsessed with the baby, as I've sometimes seen, which means strains on the baby as well as on the parents and sometimes the parent's relatives and friends. (p. 175)

The real experts: Parents

Parents reading books of expert advice do so for a reason. They want to improve their parenting in order to raise children who are healthy, happy, and functional members of society. In reading such books, however, they may be influenced to make changes to the way in which their family works which might have a negative impact on the functioning of the family and the child. The authors of such books, in taking on the role of the expert (the qualifications of the expert-author are generally displayed on the front cover), and providing generic advice to parents in such a way are, in essence, interfering with and disrupting the unique and natural relationships the child has within the family. This negative impact is increased exponentially when the author promotes views which are out of context, diminish the child, and/or simplify family relationships.

But what is the alternative to following such advice, particularly as many parents seek it out of feelings of inadequacy? Given the pressures on parents to produce children who conform to wider societal expectations (Bornstein, 2005), it is hardly surprising that they feel that they might be doing something wrong. The answer might lie in the promotion of greater empowerment for parents, combined with a recognition that under normal circumstances (and with the exception of severely dysfunctional or abusive situations) family relationships should not be critiqued in terms of what is correct and what is not correct, especially as this critique has not been invited by the subjects. According to Mason (2005), in her discussion of supporting parents with disabilities to look after their own children 'the bigger question concerns the change in society which is making the raising of children more difficult and lonelier for everyone . . . parenting is a relationship, not a job . . . [and] resources are best put to supporting that relationship' (p. 22). Part of the problem is the trend for politicians and the media to blame parents for what is wrong with society and to expect them to fix the problem. According to Moran and Ghate (2005)

> To judge by the attention given to parenting by UK policymakers in recent years, you could be forgiven for thinking there were few headlining social problems – from anti-social behaviour on our streets to childhood obesity and falling standards in schools – for which 'better parenting' was not the solution. (p. 329)

Parents need to be reassured that they know what is best for their child, and a reduction in forms of media involving experts unnecessarily blaming parents in books marketed to them would be one step on the path to achieving this. Power relationships exist between professionals and parents (Young, 1999), and acknowledging and exploring the basis of such power relationships might be beneficial. In examining the basis on which some professionals are considered to be experts, parents might come to value their own expertise and judgement more. Parents know their children better than any remote expert, and generalizations about children made by authors such as Borba, Mamen, and Sears and Sears tend to reduce parenting to a series of simplistic recipes which can rarely serve to genuinely support the complexities of children and families interacting in varied contexts. Another step in the right direction might be for public figures and the media to stop pandering to the largely inaccurate and unsupported populist perception that certain styles of parenting are at the heart of many of the social problems apparent today. Parents might then feel more comfortable to interact with their children in more authentic and natural ways.

New technologies, new pressures

Child–family relationships have also come under strain from sources other than expectations from adults in society. Changes in the way people live, work, and interact in the twenty-first century have placed pressures on family relationships which were not as evident only 20 years ago. The increasing prevalence of communication technology in the home now plays its part in devaluing and reducing the amount and quality of family interactions, and so has an impact on family relationships. This technology has become pervasive in the daily lives of many people, the most notable forms being land-line telephones, mobile telephones (often with text messaging), Blackberry style PDAs, video games, computers and the internet, and television. A recent study found that children spend increasing amounts of time using screen media as they grow up. Jordan, Hersey, McDivitt, and Heitzler (2006) found that children aged 6–7 spend nearly 4 hours per day using screen media. Children aged 9–10 spend nearly 6 hours, and children aged 12–13 spend nearly 6.5 hours per day using screen media. The use of such technology for work and leisure in the daily lives of all family members has obstructed valuable face-to-face interactions between children and their families.

The impact of television on family life has been documented for many years now, and with this medium now being considered old technology recent studies are less common. However, what is clear is that television continues to get in the way of personal interaction between family members. The time dedicated to children's television viewing alone is reason for concern. In the United States, Woodard (2000) found that children spend over 3 hours per day on average watching television. Relationships between children and other family members are often harmed by or built around television viewing habits (DeGaetano, 2005). Television is, however, a feature of modern life that will likely remain for the foreseeable future. And it is not all bad. Television can be instructive, and it is a means of cultural transmission.

Wright et al. (2001) found that children who watched educational-style children's shows between the ages of two and three demonstrated subsequent high performance on tests of reading, receptive vocabulary, math, and general school readiness, especially when compared with children who viewed less educational shows. What is precarious is the balance of time devoted to meaningful, face-to-face personal family relationships, compared to screen time with the television.

While television impacts family relationships, it now faces competition from newer forms of communication technology. Internet access is becoming increasingly common in homes globally, and even children at very young ages are spending considerable amounts of time using the internet at home and at school. It has been estimated that by 2011, 44.3 per cent of children in the United States aged 3–11 will use the internet at least once a month, and that at the end of September 2007, 86.6 per cent of internet users spent more than 6 hours a week online (eMarketer, 2007). The time that children and families dedicate to the internet each day alone should give us pause, however, some research suggests the impact of internet usage reaches beyond time issues, and directly impacts the nature and quality of personal relationships between children and other family members. Leung (2007) examined the relationship between stressful life events and internet use in 717 children and adolescents aged 8–18. He found a significant association between stressful life events and internet consumption for the purposes of mood management (e.g. playing games to make oneself feel better) and social compensation, such as gaining recognition or maintaining relationships with others. The levels of social support found online helped reduce the impact of stressful life events. Interestingly, Leung found that off-line social support also helped reduce the impact of stressful events, but the more the subjects were able to personally access means of social support, the more likely they were to turn to the internet for mood management and social compensation. Children, then, appear to be increasingly turning to the online world for support in times of stress as opposed to the equally effective approach of turning to someone in the real-world environment. These more personal supports who might in the past have been family members or close friends are in the process of being replaced by the online technological environment. Cyber-relationships are still relationships, and certainly have value, however, it can be safely assumed that children on the internet are generally not communicating with their immediate families, and in any event cyber-relationships are different from face-to-face relationships (Kang, 2007). Family becomes less of a forum for discussing problems and seeking support. As such, the importance of the role of the family, so valued by UNESCO and the UN as the fundamental unit of society, is diminished.

Parents, however, are left with few options for reclaiming face-to-face family time and relationships when it comes to communication technology and screens. Studies by Sook-Jung and Young-Gil (2007) discussed below highlight the apparent futility of parental efforts to reduce screen time and take back family time. A compromise position is seemingly the only option. If we acknowledge that communication technology has an impact on family relationships, and therefore the level of respect for children and their need for such relationships, then efforts must be made to ameliorate the impact of these technologies. Families need to answer themselves on the question of how much is too much when it comes to communication technology use in the home, but they likely need to do this collaboratively. Children, as family members, need to be a part of the decision-making process. The internet abounds with practical suggestions on how to reduce overall screen time for children (such as reduced numbers of television sets in each household), however these suggestions will only be useful if families commit to valuing face-to-face relationships and reflect together on how to take back that time in a reasonable and pragmatic manner.

Window on Research

Sook-Jung and Young-Gil (2007) examined the impact of children's internet use on family time and relationships in Korea. They conducted an in-class survey on a sample of 222 children in Grades 4–6 (two classes from each grade level) to try and find out if declines in family time and communication result from children's internet use, and the relationship between parental mediation of the internet and children's online activities. A computer with internet access at home was available to 92.8 per cent of the children in the survey. Sook-Jung and Young-Gil used an instrument which combined frequency reporting of time spent on specific online activities and other demographic variables, along with questions using a Likert scale.

They found a relationship between time spent on the internet by children and perceived declines in family time, however the children felt that family communication was not negatively impacted by internet use because the technology displaced passive family time rather than active communication time. They also found that depending on the type of online activities children engaged in, the impact on family time and communication differed. For example, family relationships were not threatened by

> ### Window on Research—cont'd
>
> using the internet for reasons of completing homework or searching for educational information. However, using the internet for communication and chat with others was associated with a decline in family relationships.
>
> They also found that parent restrictions on internet usage were generally ineffective, however children were more likely to engage in educational online activities if parents recommended useful websites to them, and/or engaged in co-using the internet with them.

Respecting children's relationships and family life at school

To this point the majority of this chapter has focused on relationships between parents and children: family life. This theme will continue to be evident in the following discussion, however greater emphasis will now be given to other types of relationships children have. These commonly occur in, although are not limited to, the school setting. These relationships include child–peer relationships, and child–teacher relationships which could both to be said to occur within the context of Bronfenbrenner's (1979) microsystem. The discussion will also be broadened to include relationships between teachers and parents which might be said to occur in the mesosystem, or even the exosystem (depending on how you view them). Teacher–parent relationships can have a profound impact on the quality of a child's overall experience when it comes to their own personal relationships at school, and so form an essential part of the discussion in this domain.

Egocentrism and social relationships

The traditional developmental view of young children is that they are primarily egocentric, and that their capacity for empathy and relationships with others have limits (Ormrod, Saklofske, Schwean, Harrison, & Andrews, 2006). According to Rodd (1997) young children's egocentrism means they are less capable of negotiating social relationships or seeing points of view which conflict with their own. If we accept this observation, we accept also that egocentric children might have more difficulty functioning in learning situations requiring social reciprocity. For decades teacher preparation programmes have promoted this view, creating a body of educators with these beliefs about children. These beliefs have influenced educators' relationships with children. However, the theorist who brought the idea of egocentrism during childhood into popular use, Jean Piaget (1929, 1952), insisted that his idea was commonly misinterpreted. According to Favre and Bizzini (1995), 'In the Piagetian view, children go from egocentric thinking to increasingly decentred modes of thought, characterized by their growing ability to take on another's point of view, and to consider the same reality from different sides in a coordinated way' (p. 18). As children get older and their thinking becomes more complex, higher demands are placed on this move towards greater decentration of thought. The more widely accepted idea of egocentric children conjures up ideas of selfishness, and a lack of concern for others and for relationships. But this was not Piaget's view. According to a later clarification by Piaget (1959; cited also in Favre & Bizzini)

> Sociability and egocentrism in no way exclude each other. The egocentric mind is, in fact, far more susceptible to suggestions from outside and the influence of the group than a mind which has been disciplined by cooperation; in so far as it does not know itself, the egocentric mind cannot become conscious of its own personality. (p. 277)

Piaget's work unintentionally created a misperception about childhood egocentrism, and this has continued to the present day despite the later clarifications. This misperception, however, is now increasingly being challenged by those who have followed Piaget. Rinaldi (2006) argues that egocentrism should be seen as disorientation rather than a persistent and consistent focus on the self. In this view, children are capable of social relationships and putting others first if problems are contextualized for them. When they see the impact an action may have on others they are willing to modify their action, even if it might disadvantage themselves. Kravtsova (2006) provides a description of working with children in this way, which lends support to the idea of the disoriented child

> To ensure that a child's promised behavior coincides with his actual behavior, it is essential to focus his attention as often as possible on the feelings and desires of other people, to discuss the reasons other people do what they do, and to discuss possible alternative behaviour in some situation. When a person understands what factors motivate behavior, including his own behaviour, and has the ability to put himself in the place of others, it becomes possible to build relationships with others, to avoid conflicts, and to establish interaction based on trust. (p. 79)

Others, including Newcombe and Huttenlocher (1992), and Siegler (1998), have also questioned the notion of egocentrism in the commonly understood sense of the word. This would likely sit well with Piaget, who only ever intended his work in this area to serve as a framework to be filled in by others (Lorenco & Machado, 1996). Take, for example, a case study of toddlers Lorenzo and Matilde (Bonetti & Filippini, 2001; cited also in Loreman, 2007a). In this story two toddlers at the age of 20 months (an age during which they would traditionally be thought to be primarily egocentric) socially negotiate the solution to a problem of getting a desired rock out of a tight space in the playground. Matilde enlists the help of Lorenzo to problem solve the situation, and the two children work together to retrieve the rock. Lorenzo helps his friend for its own sake (there is little personal benefit), and Matilde has demonstrated signs of thinking of others and calling on her pre-established social relationships for assistance. It is easy to disregard this learning experience as being insignificant, or to diminish the relationship as immature or cute, however the complexity inherent in children's relationships such as these needs to be recognized, even when they are very young. If this is possible at the age of 20 months, then certainly it happens at the school age. This points to the positive impact that respecting and encouraging social relationships between children in formal learning settings such as schools can have on learning. Ideally, educators need to correct their views about what egocentrism is. In doing so they will come to the conclusion that egocentrism and child–peer relationships are not mutually exclusive. This may result in more attempts by educators to reorient children to see the point of view of others in the way described by Rinaldi (2006) above, which can only serve to improve child–peer relationships.

Classroom structures and practices which respond to the need for relationships

Educators can also respond to the need for relationships in learning in a number of other ways. First, the physical structure and the nature of educational activities in schools can be structured in such a way as to promote social relationships. Traditionally, classrooms have seated children in desks in rows, with all eyes towards the teacher at the front of the room (Loreman, Deppeler, & Harvey, 2005). These sorts of structures are designed to minimize student interactions and maximize attention at the front of the room, along with perceptions of the authority of the teacher. The child's natural desire for relationships with his or her peers is discouraged in these circumstances. If these relationships are to be valued and respected, then structures in class-rooms similar to these are to be avoided. Teachers who operate according to a social constructivist perspective (see Vygotsky, 1978) tend not to structure their classrooms in this way. Their aim is to encourage interaction; to build relationships. Because of this, they might group children differently for learning; for example in groups at tables where discussion with peers is easier. Obviously, changing seating arrangements is fairly rudimentary and is only a beginning, used here as just one example. Any number of modifications to the traditional classroom set-up can and should be made where they are consistent with promoting and encouraging relationships between children.

Consideration also needs to be given to the expectations for conduct while learning at school. The notion of having children spend long periods of the school day working in silence is favoured by some educators because it demonstrates that they are in control of the class, and also awards certain gravity to the activity being undertaken. However, if one were to encounter a group of 25 adults who saw each other each day, and who worked in close proximity to one another conducting their activities in silence, this would seem very unusual. One would expect these adults to be communicating both about the task at hand, as well as engaging in small talk. For an employer, for instance, to demand that these adults work in silence would in normal circumstances be seen as demeaning. Having children work in silence at their desks, however, seems a perfectly normal thing in some classrooms. Children need to be permitted to communicate with one another because they have relationships with each other, and a teacher's fear that this will distract them from important work is only valid if they value individual achievement on narrow tasks more than learning in the context of relationship, negotiation, and social reciprocity. Of course, a chaotic, excessively noisy classroom where others are unable to effectively communicate is not respectful of relationships either, and children need to learn what an appropriate level of volume for classroom communications is if they do not know already. This, however, is a relatively minor detail and is easily addressed for those who want to foster positive relationships in their classroom.

The third main feature of a classroom that respects children's relationships with each other relates to the sorts of activities children are engaged in. A heavy reliance on individual tasks denies children's right to relationships as they learn and is not consistent with social constructivist pedagogy. Instead, a classroom which respects child–peer relationships is one in which children are primarily engaged in tasks that foster their own individual learning and competencies within a group context. Instead of having children measure the width of their classrooms by themselves, they might measure the entire school in a group activity which involves planning, evaluating, social negotiation, and other skills, in addition to the measurement of length. This would respect the social nature of children and learning, and promote a focus on cooperation, community, and personal competence rather than individual achievement. This community focus is more apparent in some non-European cultures. For example, First Nations people in North America survived in harsh environments thanks to a system of communal sharing of skills and abilities. Even today Cree children will innocently engage in behaviours those from European backgrounds might consider cheating, such as getting the answers to a question in class from a friend. For many children this is not cheating, but rather an instance of cultural misunderstanding; sharing the correct answers, which are seen as communal knowledge, is positive in their eyes. Many Cree children do not understand why you would not tell your friend the answer if he or she does not know it. The focus is on community and relationship rather than individual achievement (Collins, 2005).

Productive home–school relationships

Schools also tend to be environments in which a clear delineation is drawn between activities which some perceive should take place in educational settings, and those which take place at home. Despite the fact that many schools now say that they involve families as partners in the learning process, in practical terms this is rarely actually the case. This tends to devalue another aspect of relationship; relationships between child, family, and school. Relationships between educators and children, and educators and parents, tend to take on a formal or at least semi-formal tone. Most codes of professional conduct set by teacher professional associations highlight the expectation that teachers will conduct themselves in a professional manner in their interactions with others, including colleagues, children, and parents (see e.g. the Victorian Institute of Teaching, 2007). Professional codes of conduct are important because to some degree they ensure that inappropriate interactions between educators and others do not occur, as relationships are always to be conducted through the veneer of guarded professionalism. There is, however, no alternative. Quite simply, teachers must and should behave according to professional standards.

Having said that, the idea of professional interactions between educators and others does not imply that these relationships need to be cold and clinical. They can and need to be warm, caring, empathetic, respectful, contextually relevant, and understanding. This, however, is unfortunately not always the case. While there is an abundance of literature and school policy which recognizes the importance of school–family partnerships, instances of true partnership and collaboration are far less common. Baker, Kessler-Sklar, Piotrkowski, and Lamb Parker (1999) found that 190 kindergarten and first-grade teachers in 65 US schools had limited knowledge of the sort of involvement parents had in the education of their children. This finding is consistent with the view that despite the stated desirability of parent–school collaborations, the reality is that there are limited opportunities for meaningful dialogue and involvement. These opportunities are arguably limited because many schools and homes have not worked together to create them. In the United Kingdom, Ravet (2007) examined perceptions of disengagement in primary classrooms. This study found some views in common about the reasons for disengagement between parents and children, but these views were not shared by teachers. Ravet concludes that this lack of understanding gets in the way of meaningful teacher–child interactions in the classroom, and accounts for poor relationships and the breakdown in teaching and learning for those children who are disengaged at school.

Ravet's study is important because it outlines the consequences of continuing to engage in fractured relationships. In order to respect a child's broader relationships, any artificial barriers which exist between the home and the school need to be removed. A positive example of what this relationship might look like if parents were more a part of schools comes from Kyriakides (2005) who investigated an instance of promising practice in Cyprus. His study examined the attempts of a primary school to implement a policy whereby parents participated in working directly with their children in classrooms in the context of the regular school day. Using a similar school not implementing this policy as a control group, Kyriakides found that after only six months children in the school in which parents were involved demonstrated comparatively higher attainment in not only core academic areas, but also in a variety of other non-core areas. What is important in terms of relationships, however, and probably more significant that academic improvement, is that both parents and students developed positive attitudes towards this partnership policy, and parents indicated that their involvement in the classroom contributed significantly to improved teacher communication and also to student behaviour at home. The mutual benefits of authentic home–school partnerships are evident in this study, and variations on this theme might be explored by schools and families wanting to build closer, more productive relationships for the benefit of children.

Case Study: Grandma's Christmas Visit

After spending two weeks over Christmas with her daughter, son-in-law, and two grandchildren, a 65-year-old grandmother said the following 'I don't understand parents today. They seem to like to make life difficult for themselves and it doesn't seem to make the slightest bit of difference with the children. My daughter and her husband run themselves ragged and bend over backwards for their kids. The baby spends almost every night sleeping in their bed. My daughter says that this helps with bonding, and also produces more secure and confident adults in the future. From what I can see, nobody is getting any sleep. My daughter hardly ever puts the baby down during the day, and breastfeeds frequently because she read somewhere she should do this. Granted, the baby is fussy, but in my day the solution was to put them in their cot and let them scream it out. They soon stopped.

The 3-year-old really knows how to get what he wants. If he doesn't want to eat his dinner he simply begins crying, and his parents go and get him an alternate meal. In fact, the family rarely sits down to a common meal because special foods are always prepared for the children in advance. My grandson barely ever plays by himself. Both his parents are constantly playing games with him, or chasing him around the house cleaning up after him as they also try to do all the other tasks they need to get done in their adult lives. He never puts away his own toys, his father just does it once he is in bed. Their approach to discipline is to not discipline because they say it will hurt his creativity and self-esteem. Also, he is not immunized because they read on the internet that this increases the risk of Autism. I asked my doctor about this who told me this is not true. I wonder now if he might contract some horrible disease? Things were a lot different in my day, I can tell you. Kids did what they were told or else! They had more respect. We didn't have any internet or books to tell us how to be a parent. We took the advice of our own parents and our doctor. We didn't do any of this silly negotiating with the kids, or time-outs or whatever. No, we simply told kids to do what we wanted and they did it! Don't like your dinner? Too bad, eat it anyway' (Name withheld, personal communication, 2008).

- Contrast the differences between the two different ideas about parenting. Which is the more effective and in what respect?
- Consider ideas presented earlier in this chapter regarding the promotion of inter-dependence rather than independence in children. Are there any links between these ideas and the situation presented in this case study?

This chapter has discussed some, but obviously not all, of the aspects of relationships and children. One view of children which has considerable currency is that they are not independent islands. Consideration must be given to the idea that they exist in the context of a network of fluid relationships which shift and change according to time and any number of other factors. Respecting childhood involves recognition of the existence, complexity, interrelatedness, and importance of these relationships along with a commitment to ensuring that all participants in these relationships are cared for, supported, valued, and nurtured.

Discussion Questions

- Consider further Bronfenbrenner's (1979) idea of the chronosystem (the idea that patterns and experiences that tend to occur and reoccur over the lifespan). How might it impact the other ecological systems he identified?
- Review a popular psychology guidebook for parents. What features promote greater respect for children and childhood?
- Examine your own habits with respect to use of communication technologies. Do they impact face-to-face relationships in your life?
- What instances of parent involvement have you seen in schools? In what respects would you consider these to be truly collaborative, meaningful partnerships?

Further Resources

Bronfenbrenner, U. (1979). *The ecology of human development: Experiments by nature and design*. Cambridge, MA: Harvard University Press.

Kyriakides, L. (2005). Evaluating school policy on parents working with their children in class. *Journal of Educational Research*, *98*(5), 281–98.

Nimmo, J. (1998). The child in community: Constraints from the early childhood lore. In C. Edwards, L. Gandini, & G. Forman (eds). *The hundred languages of children: The Reggio Emilia approach – advanced reflections*. Connecticut, USA: Ablex Publishing.

4

Respecting Children's Capacities and Abilities

Introduction

This chapter further examines ideas about competency, especially as it relates to children's capacities and abilities. It questions some of the traditional views about children's capacities and abilities in light of growing recognition that children are endowed with the means to be creative, flexible, open-minded thinkers, capable of making sound judgements and constructing knowledge in complex ways.

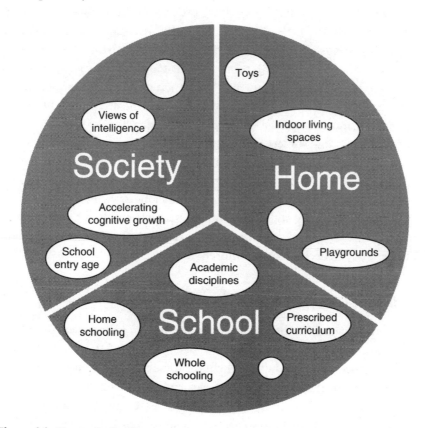

Figure 4.1 Chapter outline figure

The big picture

Childhood is often represented in condescending ways, especially through the media. Television shows regularly feature children acting predominantly silly or cute, and similar advertisements capitalize on children's naïve responses to adult situations. These situations amuse, in part, because there is 200-year-old heritage of viewing children as innocent, intellectually unaware, and pure (Seichepine, 2004). These representations of children continue because there is some truth to the idea that children often respond to new situations by questioning some aspects adults might consider self-evident. This, however, likely results from lack of experience in the adult world, rather than any reduced intellectual capacity on the part of a child. It is tempting to view this questioning as naïvety rather than a demonstration of a child's robust natural learning process. Groth's (2007) view is that 'very young boys and girls alike are physically weak and socially incompetent' (p. 10). While children are obviously physically weak if compared to adults (an unfair comparison), robust intellect and complex social thinking are evident in what children are able to learn and do in the space of the few years since their birth. Consider that by 6 years most children have mastered one (or more) language, have started to learn how to read, count and add numbers, know something about their local communities, have been involved in a variety of physical activities, have participated in music and art, have conducted their own informal scientific experiments and come to some conclusions, and have developed competencies in negotiating social relationships. Yet many adults continue to perceive children as being essentially rudimentary, black and white thinkers, and neglect to see the legitimate, serious intellectual work children do.

Traditional views of intelligence

Some of this negativity has roots in traditional, uni-dimensional views of intelligence. Intelligence (IQ) tests have been developed to try and quantify the intelligence of both adults and children, but have been found wanting. A full critique of the many problems associated with intelligence testing is beyond the scope of this text (for a plain-language treatment of the topic please refer to Richardson, 1999), however, it should be noted that these tests have been developed in the absence of any clear agreement on exactly what intelligence is. A 1921 issue of the *Journal of Educational Psychology* that followed a symposium in which the leading psychologists of the day submitted their definitions of intelligence, failed to find common ground. A similar symposium in the year 1986 yielded like results, and indeed moved the debate even further away from a simple definition (Sternberg & Berg, 1986). Intelligence tests, then, were not devised based on an agreed notion of what needed to be tested, but rather were developed in close partnership with school teachers (Richardson, 1999). Given this, it comes as no surprise that IQ tests contain largely school-type tasks of a fairly narrow, traditionally academic nature favouring literacy and logical-mathematical thinking. However, as a clear definition of intelligence eludes us, it is not possible to construct a test which will measure it. The best we can say is that a person's performance on an IQ test measures performance on the test compared to other people, and this is not necessarily intelligence. That there is a correlation between test perfor-mance and school performance means little; the tests were, after all, devel-oped with the cooperation of teachers.

The simplicity of IQ tests, the quantification of what many still view as intelligence in a single number – an IQ score – has been used as a means for viewing children's capacities and abilities in very narrow and often negative ways. Even where children are not formally tested, the uni-dimensional view of intelligence promoted by the heritage of IQ testing results in environments for children where performance in traditional areas of literacy (often viewed as mostly reading and writing) and numeracy are valued above all else. The extent of children's capacities and abilities are viewed in that context, and limited by it.

Alternate views of intelligence

Howard Gardner (1983, 1999) provided us with an alternate view of intel-ligence which is useful in helping to see the true extent of the richness and complexity of children's (indeed everyone's) capacities and abilities. To Gardner, intelligence is not a single, static entity. His view is that intelligence is multidimensional, comprising different strands which both interact with one another and develop at different rates and to differing extents depending on the individual. His multiple intelligences are shown in Table 4.1.

Gardner's theory is useful in that it allows us to view the many areas in which children can be intelligent, and can develop and demonstrate their capacities and abilities. Where IQ tests assume innate, essentially unchang-ing levels of ability, the multiple intelligences assume natural capacities in some areas, but also the possibility for development (becoming more intel-ligent) in some or all areas. While Gardner dabbled in the development of some tests which might produce a useful profile of a child's strengths and interests in the various intelligences he identified, he 'would prefer to spend more resources helping learners understand and develop their individual

Table 4.1 Howard Gardner's Multiple Intelligences

Intelligence	Description
Verbal-linguistic	Language-based activities such as reading, speaking, writing, dramatic presentations
Musical	Reading and writing music, music appreciation, playing instruments
Bodily-kinesthetic	Athletic and sporting abilities, dance, yoga, skill in physical activities
Interpersonal	Social skills, discerning the moods, feelings, desires of others, and responding appropriately
Mathematical-logical	Number-based activities, use of logic and reasoning, mathematical thinking
Naturalistic	Awareness of the plant and animal world. Growing plants, raising animals, training animals
Visual-spatial	Awareness of space, relational aspects of space, representing space in models and diagrams. Relationship to fine arts endeavours
Existential	Esoteric knowledge, spirituality, intuition, philosophical
Intrapersonal	Awareness of ones own performances, capacities and abilities in different areas. Reflective and metacognitive features

intelligence profiles and spend less resources testing, ranking, and labelling them' (Gardner & Moran, 2006, p. 230). Gardner's position has been that he is not interested in any profile developed by others being used as some kind of formal achievement scale, but rather as a working indicator of a child's capacities and abilities in any given area. Knowledge of the multiple intelligences is intended to be a catalyst for the promotion of more advanced learning in the identified areas. This is a respectful way of viewing children's capacities and abilities; the areas in which they are intelligent are many, and all can be further developed. Under Gardner's model children are likely multi-talented, and have the capacity to build on those talents.

School entry age: Strategizing to get an edge

Another element of respecting children's capacities and abilities relates to educational contexts, which are particularly crucial for those of a young age. Children have traditionally been involved in relatively few formal adult-structured learning contexts much before the age at which they would normally attend school. This practice, however, has recently come under some pressure. More informal, play-based, and child-directed environments such as pre-schools, day care, or the home are in some cases being abandoned in favour of more formal, sometimes elitist, educational and school environments at younger and younger ages than ever before (Wallingford & Prout, 2000). Some parents pursue this in the belief that it will provide their children with an educational advantage over their peers. For the same reasons, some parents hold their children back from school beyond the age at which they might normally attend. In that way, the belief is, the more mature child will have learned advanced skills and will therefore have an advantage over his or her less mature classmates (Graue & DiPerna, 2004). School is the main context in which this age manipulation (or redshirting) occurs, however, it can equally be applied to situations in which children are placed in highly structured sporting, musical, artistic, or any other form of learning endeavour at an early age in order to provide them with an edge over their peers. This practice does a disservice to the capacities and abilities of children for two reasons. First, even if it is unspoken in front of the child, it places them in situations in which they are at least implicitly in competition with other children. Secondly, this sort of fast-forwarding disregards children's natural cognitive and emotional developmental capacities, and their need for learning through play. The practice is as ineffective as it is potentially damaging. Research (cited and discussed below) shows that children benefit from growing in environments (home, in the community, or in a pre-school) with their same-age peers, rather than with markedly older or younger children in the more rigidly structured environment, such as is a feature of most formal educational settings. Parents who place their child into school sooner than is usual often rationalize the practice in terms of providing their child with the edge to succeed in a society which is competitive and values individualism. In promoting individual success at the expense of others, these parents devalue the arguably desirable interdependent relationships with peers which have been discussed in the previous chapter.

Accelerating cognitive development

Theories about children's intellectual growth and development have made strong contributions in support of the idea that accelerating cognitive development in children is not possible. The most influential theorist, Piaget (1970), promoted views about children's capacities which have had a significant negative impact on the way children's development is perceived. The structuralist aspects of Piaget's work, often supported by later research, demonstrate the futility of trying to accelerate cognitive development. In his theory, Piaget outlined four developmental stages. In the sensory motor stage (from birth to 2 years) children interact and begin to make meaning of their world via the information they receive through the five senses. They grasp, suck, hear, see, and taste what is around them, and as they progress through this stage their actions become more intentional. In the preoperational stage (2–6 or 7 years) children begin to use language in more social ways, and engage in more symbolic and representational forms of play. Thinking in this stage is egocentric (in the Piagetian sense of the word), and often simple in that they are generally able to only see one aspect of a problem or situation. In the concrete operational stage (age 6 or 7 to about 12 years) children engage in more organized and logical thought. They become able to solve concrete problems in logical ways (often needing to use manipulatives), but continue to think largely in black and white terms. In the formal operational stage (age eleven or twelve and above) children are able to engage in more complex abstract thought, and see problems and issues from multiple perspectives. They are able to more readily present hypotheses and solve problems with less concrete processes. Piaget argued that children will progress through each of these stages not according to a strict timeline of chronological ages, but rather according to meeting four criteria which are: sufficient experience, social interaction, equilibration (or cognitive balance), and maturation. It is primarily the criteria of maturation which precludes children moving more quickly through the cognitive stages. This refers to biological maturation. Quite simply, brains will grow and develop according to their own schedule, not ours.

Research on school entry age

Studies support Piaget's structuralist views on maturation by showing that at best there are no long-term benefits of sending children to school earlier or later than is usual. Indeed, the practice can be harmful. Kavkler, Aubrey, and Tancig (2000) found that by age eight any academic advantages in mathematics achievement realized by early school starters ceased to exist. Morton and Courneya (1990) found a positive correlation between children labelled with learning disabilities and those who had been early school starters. Even in their control group they found a positive correlation between low achievers not formally labelled as learning disabled and early school starters. Wallingford and Prout (2000), using a sample of 1,222 children, also identified a trend of significantly higher levels of referral to special education services of children who started school at a younger age. In terms of delaying a child's entry to school so that they are older in comparison to their peers Byrd, Weitzman, and Auinger (1997) found a positive correlation between behaviour problems and children who were older than their classmates, especially in the adolescent years. They suggested that there are latent harmful effects associated with delaying children's school entry. May and Kundert (1995) also found that children who entered school a year later than usual were placed in special education programmes in significantly higher proportions when compared with their peers who had entered school at the usual age. This research is clear. Sending children to school at ages not consistent with the standard age at which their peers attend school is not beneficial, and is most probably harmful. One element of respecting children's capacities and abilities is to keep them out of formal school settings, or putting them in school, at an appropriate age.

Window on Research

Lawson and Wollman (2003) examined the transition from Piaget's concrete to formal stage of cognitive functioning. Specifically, they investigated if training could accelerate this transition (seen as the ability to isolate and control variables) in terms of specific and more generalized tasks. They studied 32 Grade 5 and 32 Grade 7 students in California, ranging in age from 9.5 to 12.1 years with normal IQs ranging from 100–115. An experiment was conducted in which a 16-student control group was established at each grade level. The other 16 students at each grade level received training involving solving problems with cause-and-effect relationships by isolating and controlling variables. A pre- and post-test was conducted to see if there was any difference in the groups who had the training compared to the control groups.

The study found that training resulted in better performance on specific and more novel formal operational tasks for both the Grade 5 and Grade 7 groups, however there was no significant difference between the trained and control groups when it came to generalizing formal operational thinking to other contexts. This shows that while training can help to advance children towards formal operational thinking in some specific areas, it is limited in its extent. This to some degree supports the argument that biological maturation is necessary for genuine, comprehensive movement between the Piaget's concrete and formal operational stages. Lawson and Wollman (2003) suggest, however, that training in formal operational-type activities is useful for children in the concrete operational stage because it does have an impact on their attainment of formal operational thinking, and will also help to ensure that a child's progress from one stage to another is not unnecessarily hindered or delayed.

Respecting children's capacities and abilities at home

Respectful interior physical environments

The fostering of environments that will nurture a child's abilities and capacities in cognitive, physical, emotional, and spiritual ways is paramount. The environments in which we allow children to live their lives reflect our levels of respect for their individual variations and capacities. However, Tarr (2001, 2004) argues that many of the commercially available decorations for classroom walls (and, it can be assumed, other contexts, including the home) serve to silence children rather than acknowledging and promoting their creativity. Describing one classroom which was visually busy with commercial materials on the walls and hanging from the ceiling, Tarr (2004) observed that 'Almost mute amid the visual din were children's drawings and written work on the walls' (p. 88). Tarr goes on to say that

> The image of the learner embedded in these materials is that of a consumer of information who needs to be entertained, rather than a child who is curious and capable of creating and contributing to the culture within this environment. (p. 89)

The alternative to this is the maintenance or creation of more enabling environments for children. Posters of cartoon characters on bedroom or classroom walls can be replaced by children's own creative efforts which would demonstrate a higher regard for their products. Ceppi and Zini (1998) led a team of Italian researchers examining children's spaces and their relationships with these spaces. This project deconstructed some exemplary pre-school environments and examined what is important in terms of lighting, colour, furniture, functionality, and other aspects of overall design. The implications of this study reach beyond the pre-school and into all environments in which children spend time. Rinaldi (1998), in summing up the project, concludes that

> The objective is thus to construct and organize spaces that enable children:
>
> - to express their potential, abilities, and curiosity;
> - to explore and research alone and with others, both peers and adults;
> - to perceive themselves as constructors of projects and of the overall educational project carried out in the school;

- to reinforce their identities (also in terms of gender), autonomy, and security;
- to work and communicate with others;
- to know that their identities and privacy are respected. (p. 120)

Bruner (1998) adds that a pre-school needs to be somewhere 'where the young discover the uses of mind, of imagination, of materials, and learn the power of doing these things together. It is as much like a stage, a self-made museum, or a forum as it is a classroom' (p. 137). This idea of an environment which respects children's capacity to create could be said to be a requirement of any of the spaces children regularly inhabit, including the home and public spaces in the community.

Respectful exterior physical environments

Views that children have limited abilities and capacities are reflected in more than wall decorations and interior spaces which surround them. If, as Gandini (1998) says, the environment is itself an educator, then some exterior environments constructed especially for children provide evidence of a disrespect for children's capacities. Children's playgrounds, for example, are now usually designed so as to reduce the risk of children hurting themselves, and while these design changes have been effective in reducing playground injuries (Howard et al., 2005), caution needs to be exercised when modifying existing playgrounds or building new ones. While nobody would advocate unsafe playgrounds for children (in the United States 205,000 playground injuries are treated annually; see American School & University, 2007), the creation of sterile, limiting environments where children can engage in few other activities than swinging or sliding above rubber mats leaves little room for experimentation and adventure. The fundamental idea behind the design and construction of such playgrounds is that children are clumsy, weak, and incapable of good judgement. Therefore, environments must be created in which such judgements do not need to be made. Furthermore, the real reason behind the construction of such playgrounds may be adult rather than child-oriented. McKendrick, Bradford, and Fielder (2000) argue that in some instances such playgrounds are constructed so as to give adults a break from children, rather than focusing on child needs and interests. Adults in these environments can relax in the knowledge that little harm can come to the children in their care, even if they are inattentive to them.

There are, however, alternatives to the creation of limiting play environments. The alternatives both reduce the risk of playground injury, and at the same time respect children's capacities to make good decisions about how they use such facilities. Schwebel (2006) found that effective adult supervision of children in playgrounds is likely the most promising means of reducing injury. The approach as suggested by Schwebel involves a component of teaching children how to use playgrounds in a safe manner, and then supporting their ability to do so. Later research demonstrated that such teaching was effective in producing behaviours likely to reduce playground injury (Schwebel, Summerlin, Bounds, & Morrongiello, 2006). Schwebel et al. focused on the playground supervisors, and promoted greater engagement with children and rewards for safe playground behaviour. In this way the adults were scaffolding (supporting) the learning for the children of safe playground behaviour. Rather than assuming children are essentially incompetent and incapable of playing safely (and therefore changing the playground to limit their play), this approach respects children's capacity to learn safe behaviour, and play in ways which would be less likely to result in injury. In an inherently unsafe world, if generalized, this approach might have positive benefits to a child's life outside the playground. It has the potential to expand the possible environments in which children can live and play.

While it is important to avoid harm, children need to be presented with opportunities to experience adventure on the playground and elsewhere, and they are certainly resilient enough to withstand a certain amount of this. Erikson (1980) argued that a certain level of challenge is important in the social and emotional development of young children. Those who do not experience some challenges which they need to overcome at a young age are less likely to be able to cope with them in a healthy way later in life. Overcoming challenges teaches children to develop their own competencies, and contributes to their notions of identity. It helps them to understand their own limitations, and if adults can help them to decide ways of possibly overcoming these limitations or alternate routes to the same goal, then a healthy attitude towards challenges and even failure to meet them can be preserved. According to Malone (2007)

> by not allowing children to engage in independent mobility and autonomous environmental play in their community, parents are denying their children important aspects of learning including psychological, social, cultural, physical and environmental. This could lead children to be lacking in environmental competence, sense of purpose, social competence, self worth and efficacy and resilience. (p. 523)

Toys to support the capable child

Playgrounds and the community are not the only contexts in which children need to be challenged. The types of toys and activities available to children in the home setting also reflect levels of respect for their capacities and abilities. Many toys on the market do little to help children develop creativity and intellectual rigour, and while inherently attractive to children, they need to be evaluated and questioned in terms of their appropriateness. Similarly, as has been discussed in Chapter 2, lengthy periods of time involved in technology use is not necessarily a desirable activity for children.

How, then, can children be occupied at home in ways which respect their inherent capabilities? The answer to that question may lie in looking to the past, back to a period where toys and technology were perhaps less available to children. Free play was a much more significant feature of a child's life 20 years ago, but this does not imply that the time was wasted. As discussed in Chapter 2, free play is an opportunity for children to engage in activities which stimulate their intellectual growth. Indeed, evidence of children's inherent capacities and abilities can be observed when they engage in free play in home, care, or pre-school environments which facilitate this.

Simply put, some toys and activities are better than others, and some toys encourage meaningful free play more than others. According to Rubin (2003) 'Like junk food, junk toys can be fun but are devoid of nutrition. Buying them requires little forethought. They are excessively commercial, and are often linked to cross-marketing schemes. They excite children at first, but that initial flicker doesn't endure.' (¶5). Good toys which encourage children to use their inherently rich capacities, abilities, and creativities do of course exist, and they are often of the low-tech variety. There is some evidence to suggest that many of the high-tech toys on the market are of little value to children, who ironically get the biggest benefit from these gadgets when using them in low-tech ways contrary to their original purpose (Ward, 2006). Examples of good toys might include the perennial staples of building blocks, modelling dough, bug catchers, art and craft materials, sand boxes, water tables, sporting equipment, and other toys which encourage experimentation and creativity. Children need to think to use these toys (some also involve healthy physical activity), and are happy to do so! Many key educational and psychological theorists have recognized the value in and encouraged the use of toys, including Locke, Froebel, Montessori, and Dewey who 'embraced the idea that toys and play could expand a child's consciousness and appetite for learning' (Ogata, 2005, p. 131). Children, then, need to engage with toys and activities which will actually serve this purpose, rather than entertaining themselves with gadgets or toys which unnecessarily restrict their natural creativity.

Window on Research

Malone and Tranter (2005) examined the impact of school playgrounds in Canberra, Australia, on play behaviours of children in two primary schools with respect to environmental learning. Using qualitative methodology, data used included behaviour mapping of play (children's movements, behaviour, and social interactions were tracked as they played), analysis of children's drawings, and interviews with children. Malone and Tranter found that there were many benefits to schools which provided areas of natural environments in which children can play. These included a reduction in aggressive school ground behaviour, a greater identification of place by children (evidence that children valued various areas in their playground), and opportunities for children to engage with formal, informal, and non-formal curricula. Malone and Tranter point out the value of providing such natural areas in school grounds for children, especially bearing in mind the increasing reticence of people to allow their children to engage in autonomous play in the community outside of school.

Respecting children's capacities and abilities at school

Reclaiming the value of the traditional scholarly disciplines

Schools are an environment in which it might be assumed that children's capacities and abilities are automatically respected given their primary purpose of facilitating learning, however, many aspects of schooling are out of step with the view that children are naturally competent, creative, co-constructors of their own learning. School curriculum in many parts of the world is evidence of this negative view of the capacities and abilities of children. The curriculum in Victoria, Australia, is in many ways representative of curricula in many countries and regions in that topics for study are predetermined, and objectives and indicators for learning are set in specific content areas. In biological science at the Grade 6 level, for example, children are expected to

6.1 Explain how ecosystems are maintained in terms of energy and matter.

6.2 Evaluate theories concerning evolution of organisms.

6.3 Describe regulation and coordination in plants and animals.

6.4 Explain cellular processes, including photosynthesis and respiration.

6.5 Describe the genetic basis of inheritance. (Victorian Curriculum and Assessment Authority, 2002, SCBS0601–5)

These sorts of learning objectives would be familiar to teachers throughout the world. The accepted rationale for such objectives is that education in the traditional learning disciplines is important. Subject disciplines exist for a reason; because over a long period of time they have been found to be important avenues of knowledge and learning. According to Gardner and Boix-Mansilla (1994)

> the scholarly disciplines represent the formidable achievements of talented human beings, toiling over the centuries, to approach and explain issues of enduring importance. Shorn of disciplinary knowledge, human beings are quickly reduced to the level of ignorant children, indeed, to the ranks of barbarians. (p. 199)

There is inherent value in the disciplines, and in children being taught by a range of teachers with discipline-specific expertise, however, what needs to be considered is the level of connection between school curriculum and the rigorous, important knowledge found in the disciplines. Gardner and Boix-Mansilla argue that the connection is often weak. School curriculum often seems a pale, superficial reflection of the rich knowledge found in the subject disciplines. Children may learn about history, for example, on a surface level of memorizing dates and events which are adequate for doing well on a test, but which may not result in the internalization of important ways of knowing and understanding history, or the types of thinking and reasoning inherent in the discipline. Curriculum presented and structured in the ways it commonly is in many parts of the world lays false claim to providing children with a robust foundation and background in the important fields of scholarship. It encourages a situation whereby schooling is structured in ways fundamentally at odds with providing children with the high quality, meaningful, and useful education they deserve.

Prescriptive curriculum missing the mark

While it is generally the responsibility of the teacher to select the pedagogical approach used to teach the material, content which is predetermined to the level it is in most western curricula makes it difficult for children to choose what they will learn, and when they are ready to learn it. Their questions about the world and their place in it go unanswered unless they coincide with the curriculum. The reality for Victorian Grade 6 teachers and children using the curriculum cited above is that during the school year children must have studied the genetic basis of inheritance. They may be able to parrot-back superficial ideas behind the notion of genetics and inheritance, but will this hold true meaning for them when presented in such a decontextualized manner? This encourages a direct, teacher-centred approach whereby educators, not children, select what is to be learned and when, with little flexibility or room for negotiation.

One response to this type of curriculum is the notion of backwards design for instruction (Wiggins & McTighe, 2005). Perhaps resigned to the reality of specific, predetermined curriculum, Wiggins and McTighe suggest that teachers identify the outcomes they want to achieve, determine the assessment that will be used, and then plan the instructional process. This type of instructional design works very well when specific objectives must be attained, however, under this model teaching and learning become an almost foregone conclusion. The avenues for open, self-directed or negotiated learning are closed because narrow targets must be met. Breaking content down into small steps that gradually become more difficult, such as is the case with curriculum structured in this way, represents a linear view of learning. Learning, however, is frequently non-linear (Doll, 1993), and children need to be given the space to manoeuvre outside of these confines.

Prescriptive, superficial, subject-based curriculum has been adopted, in part, because those who make curriculum decisions do not trust children or teachers to adequately negotiate and co-construct knowledge which will produce learning in areas which they believe will be of importance now, or, more importantly to them, in the future (see Chapter 2). The implicit belief is that children lack the competency to guide their own learning. This, however, has not been the case in some contexts where prescriptive curriculum is not used. In the municipal early childhood system in Reggio Emilia, curriculum is child-originated and teacher-framed, meaning that children come up with the ideas for direction and teachers suggest and negotiate possible projects related to those ideas (Forman & Fyfe, 1998). Clearly, the learning taking place there is every bit as rigorous and rich as the learning taking place in settings where curriculum is prescribed (or more so), and children there are learning in traditional academic areas such as math, science, and Language Arts covered by other pre-ordained curricula (Loreman, 2007a; see also Castagnetti & Vecchi, 1997).

Curriculum is organized into a linear structure because schools teach it that way, or, alternatively, schools teach that way because of the structure of the curriculum. In either case the result is the same; curriculum is generally taught in discrete subject units. This is especially evident in secondary education where children tend to move from discrete subject to discrete subject throughout the course of a day. This type of learning is artificial and contrived, as problems which are encountered in life outside of the classroom generally require the integration of different types of knowledge in order to find a solution. It is convenient for schools to capitalize on the background of teachers with specific expertise in this way, has deep historical roots, and makes school scheduling easier (Carr, 2007), but it does not reflect the reality of everyday life and requires children to think in linear ways when this may not be necessary or desirable. Such environments can be alienating, and can help to produce and sustain some of the poor learning tendencies identified by Baird (1984; and expanded on in Baird & Northfield, 1995; and Carbone, Hurst, Mitchell, & Gunstone, 1999). These include not making connections between subject material and life outside of the classroom, and a lack of external reflective thinking where no effort is made to find links between disciplines. It is because scholarly disciplines are so important that it is essential that children are provided with the optimal context in which to understand them in an authentic way, and draw links between them.

An alternative curriculum approach, and a compromise solution (for now!)

Gardner and Boix-Mansilla (1994) suggest providing children with some of the fundamental tools required for learning in the disciplines (fundamentals such as the ability to read, write, count etc.), then structuring curriculum around big ideas, essential human questions posed throughout history, such as 'Why and how do things move?' or 'What are bodies made of ?' Children would work with experts, peers, and others on projects designed to answer these and the myriad of other questions. They might engage in multidisciplinary work in the quest to answer questions, interdisciplinary work which combines and synthesizes disciplines in order to draw conclusions, or meta-disciplinary work that examines the nature of disciplinary thought itself, deconstructing the ways of knowing peculiar to one or more disciplines. True understanding is the goal, rather than knowing at a surface level. The practical application of this approach is already evident. Some schools have had success with more integrated or project-oriented approaches to curriculum delivery, often through helping children engage in the solving of multifaceted problems, or through the completion of thematic units of work (see Lee, 2007; Venville, Wallace, & Rennie, 2000). Although the transition to this model of teaching and learning can be difficult (see Meister & Nolan, 2001), educators should not view the approach as losing control of the education they are providing, but rather as a move towards sharing control with children. This involves an adult acknowledgement of and trust in children's capacities and abilities. Teachers move from being dictators prescribing what will be learned, to the role of facilitators, shaping and guiding the learning of children who are themselves active protagonists in the learning process. Schools shift from being adult-oriented institutions, where teachers make all the decisions, to places where teachers and children work together in a negotiated, vibrant, shared environment.

This alternative does not, however, solve the immediate problem of structured, often superficial curricula which teachers are generally obliged to teach. This curricula hangs like a dark cloud over more meaningful learning experiences for children, experiences which acknowledge greater levels of respect for their capacities and abilities. Ideally, this sort of curricula needs to change, however, the reality is that this will likely not occur in the immediate or even foreseeable future. How, then, might it be reconciled with a more authentic, discipline-based approach to learning, especially in the secondary schooling years where the problem seems more acute? Despite the above misgivings about the notion of backwards design outlined by Wiggins and McTighe (2005), they present a pragmatic way of addressing the disconnect between the types of curriculum teachers must teach, and a pedagogical approach based on learning through interrogating and investigating big ideas (see also McTighe, Seif, & Wiggins, 2004). Unfortunately, because these big ideas are based on curriculum they usually are not generated by children: a fundamental problem, and one which sees this suggestion move further from the situation described above by Gardner and Boix-Mansilla (1994). However, they do offer teachers a means of both teaching the disciplines in a relatively authentic way, while also meeting the needs of the curriculum. Teachers interested in implementing this approach should consult the original text as it is beyond the scope and purpose of this book, however, simply put, Wiggins and McTighe propose that teachers analyse the curriculum they need to teach, identify the big ideas which might become apparent, then construct and facilitate learning experiences which come from these big ideas, bearing in mind the need for assessment of true understanding. Conceivably a multi-, inter-, or meta-disciplinary project may arise from such a process.

The drift towards home schooling:
Is it such a bad thing?

Such changes to the way schools have traditionally operated might go some way towards ameliorating the trend towards alternative and home schooling. While curricula and school structures are not entirely to blame (there are religious and other reasons), the perception in the community that schools are not meeting the social, academic, and other needs of children is very real. Many parents remove their children from school because they feel that the only viable alternative to systems which are not adequately valuing their children's capacities and abilities is to teach them in the home context. According to Morrison (2007), under the

> conventional model, students have little or no choice in the subjects they take. What choice they do have comes in the area of electives but there, too, choices are limited by the courses offered. Students have limited freedom of movement; they must ask permission from their teacher to leave their assigned classroom, and even within the classroom students are expected to act and move as the teacher requires. (p. 42)

This, however, is not the only basis for the move towards home schooling. Some parents have a very strong confidence in their ability to provide a pedagogically excellent and relevant education for their children (Green & Hoover-Dempsey, 2007). Morrison (2007) argues that schools are not providing children with the intellectual and physical freedom they need to become truly learned citizens. She believes that 'if left unfettered, uncoerced, and unmanipulated, children will vigorously and with gusto pursue their interests, and thus learn and make meaning on their own and in concert with others' (p. 43). Morrison is not alone in this belief, citing broad support for this view ranging from the 1960s until more recently (see e.g. Dennison, 1969; Holt, 1972, 1989; Mercogliano, 1998).

Home schooling, however, has been criticized on the basis that it might not result in the level of academic rigour some claim (Lubienski, 2003), and that children who are home schooled might miss out on the important social context provided by schools (Blok, 2004; Miles, 2004). Both these arguments have been effectively countered by home-schooling supporters. Lebeda (2007) argues that schools are not the only, or even the best context in which to socialize children, quoting Zysk (1999) that it might be useful to 'Go to your local junior school, middle school, or high school, walk down the hallways, and tell me which behaviour you see that you think our son should emulate' (p. 99). Medlin (2000) reviewed the available research literature at that time and found that while more research was needed, in some areas home-schooled children were actually better socialized and more connected to the local community. Blok (2004) analysed primarily American research on the topic, and concluded that children who are home schooled differ little from their peers at school in terms of socio-emotional development. A number of studies have also supported the academic efficacy of home schooling. Jones and Gloeckner (2004) found no statistically significant differences in home-school graduates' first year college academic performance compared to regular-schooled graduates (indeed, they did a little better than their regular school peers). Wiechers and Bester (2006) found that home-schooled Grade 4 children in South Africa performed significantly better on literacy and numeracy tests than their counterparts in government schools. Blok's (2004) examination found that children who are home schooled perform better in the areas of language, mathematics, natural sciences, and social studies.

The Whole Schooling Consortium

While some families will always choose the home-schooling option, schools might be improved and become more respectful of children's capacities and abilities by adopting some of the underlying philosophical tenets of the home-schooling movement; namely, that children are capable, curriculum needs to be relevant, and pedagogy needs to be personal. The Whole Schooling Consortium in Michigan, USA, does a good job of translating many of the desires of those who support home schooling into principles which schools can adopt that might result in a more relevant and respectful education for all children. These principles, devised by Peterson and Tamor (2003), are

1. Empower citizens for democracy. Schools involve children in sharing power and decision-making in the daily life of the classroom. Democracy is an integral part of the culture of a school among children, staff, parents, and the community.
2. Include all in learning together. All children learn together across culture, ethnicity, language, ability, gender, and age.
3. Provide authentic, multi-level instruction. Instruction is designed for diverse learners. It is comprised of engaging, active, meaningful, real-world learning opportunities at multiple levels of ability, providing scaffolds and adaptations as needed.
4. Build community. A sense of community and mutual support exist within the classroom and school. When children engage in behaviours that are

challenging, it is understood that these are expressions of underlying needs of children. Staff make commitments to caring for and supporting all children.

5. Support learning. Support in learning is needed by teachers and children alike. Schools use specialized school and community resources to strengthen the general education classroom.

6. Partner with parents and community. Genuine collaboration is built between the school, families, and the community; the school is engaged in strengthening the community. In turn, the community provides guidance to engage students, parents, teachers, and others in decision-making and direction of learning & school activities.

If schools were better able to adapt their traditional ways of working to become more responsive to child needs (and therefore better respect their capacities and abilities), while at the same time retaining their important function of transmitting important bodies of knowledge and ways of thinking, then perhaps the drift towards educating children at home might be reduced. Parents might be more willing to make the choice to send their children to schools where they see them being nurtured, socialized in a positive way, and learning in ways which are relevant in terms of pedagogy and curriculum. This is a challenge which schools need to meet. While it might seem to some that schools are being asked to change too much, and that this change is unrealistic, it must be remembered that schools already operate on a firm foundation, and are staffed by experts both in pedagogy and subject matter. Change means shifting and adapting many of the existing practices and philosophies rather than, in most cases, constructing new schools literally from the ground up. The high levels of expertise in schools, when combined with expertise and input from the community, is surely enough to make any change of this nature both possible and achievable. What is needed is the desire to make this change.

Case Study: Observations from Reggio Emilia

I have been fortunate enough to have visited a number of the world-renowned municipal infant-toddler centres and pre-primary schools in Reggio Emilia, Italy. Prior to my first visit, some study combined with lectures from educators working in the system had prepared me to enter an educational environment where young children were respected and valued, with a high level of trust being placed in their competencies and abilities. I must admit, however, to being challenged by what I saw. In the

Case Study—cont'd

Atelier (art room) there were a variety of materials such as wire, small beads, glue, scissors, and much more which would have been deemed unsafe and inappropriate in many other parts of the world. I had read that in Reggio children were exposed to authentic learning environments such as these, but to actually see it with my own eyes for the first time produced for me a moment of cognitive disequilibrium and even disbelief. I had become so accustomed to seeing child friendly environments in which there was almost no possible way a child could come to even the slightest harm, even without the presence of adults. I spoke with one of the staff who reminded me that safety was of course their highest priority in Reggio, but that ensuring safety did not equate to sanitizing the environment. Instead, in Reggio they teach the children how to properly use the materials, then work with them to help ensure that this occurs. Were incidences of injury common? Apparently not. I reflected back on the schools and pre-schools I interacted with back home. In an effort to keep children safe so much had been removed, rather than adopting the Reggio approach and teaching children how to interact safely with a variety of common materials. How much richer the world of these Italian children was! Wire sculptures placed around the room. Evidence of learning. Respect for their competence was not only spoken and written about, but put into action in concrete ways.

This respect was visible throughout the spaces inhabited by the children and adults participating in the pre-primary schools and centres I visited. The playground at the Martiri di Villa Sesso pre-primary school was reminiscent of playgrounds I frequented as a child in the 1970s. It was certainly a safe environment for the children (fenced off and free of obvious hazards), however the tone of this country-style play area was one of adventure. Trees to run around, a small forest at the back, wooden forts, swings and slides to play on, wheelbarrows, sandboxes, a small pond. When properly supervised little harm could come to the children, but the potential for rich, meaningful play and interaction with the environment in an authentic way in this no frills but natural environment was in my mind much superior to the newly built, sanitized playgrounds often seen today.

- Think back to your own childhood pre-school. Were there differences or similarities to the situations in Reggio described in the above case study?
- What other ways might a learning environment demonstrate respect for a child's capacities and abilities?

This chapter has outlined some of the contemporary views of children's capacities and abilities, and how these views are evident in society, the home, and in schools. It argues that, on the whole, children's capacities and abilities are viewed in overly simplistic and negative ways, and that this view has permeated many of the environments children inhabit, and the ways in which adults live and work with them. Some alternatives, such as restructuring schools, curriculum, children's spaces, and views on what intelligence is are suggested as antidotes and ways to move forward towards contexts which are more respectful of the positive aspects of children's capacities and abilities.

Discussion Questions

- Read the article by Meister & Nolan (2001). How do you think the concerns of the educators involved in the study might be addressed?
- In what ways has our more litigious cultural climate contributed to the sanitization of children's play spaces?
- Is it possible to reconcile the sort of structured curriculum teachers are obliged to teach, and meaningful, relevant education which is child-originated?
- In what ways do the six principles of the Whole Schooling Consortium promote a more respectful view of children's capacities and abilities? How might they be applied to a school or schools you are familiar with?

Further Resources

Gardner, H. (1983). *Frames of mind: The theory of multiple intelligences.* New York: Basic Books.
Reggio Children website: www.zerosei.comune.re.it/inter/reggiochildren.htm
Whole Schooling Consortium website: www.wholeschooling.net

Respecting Children's Behaviour and Morals

Introduction

Children's behaviour and morals have been a topic of discussion for centuries. The traditional attitude has been that adults should be carefully monitoring the behaviour and moral development of children, administering punishments for poor behaviour, and rewards for good behaviour. This chapter discusses some

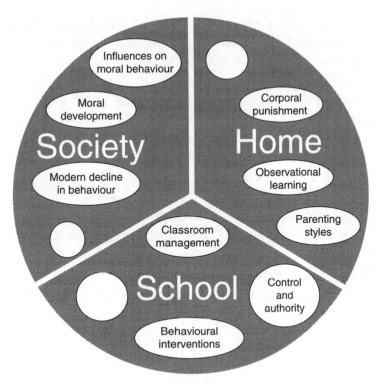

Figure 5.1 Chapter outline figure

of the issues around views about children's behaviour and morals, and provides an examination of practices that have developed to assist in producing the sorts of behaviour and moral viewpoints adults find desirable in children.

The big picture

A perception exists that children are being raised with increasingly bad manners and poor behaviour. Consider the following quote:

> Our youth now loves luxury. They have bad manners and contempt for author-
> ity. They show disrespect for elders and they love to chatter instead of exercise.
> Children are now tyrants, not the servants, of their households. They no longer
> rise when elders enter the room. They contradict their parents, chatter before com-
> pany, gobble up their food, and tyrannize their teachers. (Platt, 1989, p. 195)

This is a familiar refrain heard in much media and discourse today, however, that the above quote is attributed to Socrates in 425 BC may come as a surprise to many who may view the 'good old days' through rose-coloured glasses – as a time when children knew how to behave and showed respect for the conventions of society. It is questionable if those days ever really existed in the eyes of adults, either in Socrates time, 50 years ago, or today. The actual behaviour of children with reference to the expectations of adults has likely changed very little over time, but children being more or less physically and cognitively defenceless compared to adults are a soft target. Adults, with all the power, pass judgement on children and their behaviour, values, and morals. However, often it is not the behaviour of children which needs to be questioned, but rather the behaviour of the adults who live and work with these children, and who produce contexts in which children's behaviour is either viewed in a negative way, or becomes antisocial in actuality as a consequence of the context.

Moral development: Kohlberg's simplistic and negative view

Kohlberg (1971, 1976), for example, in his well-known theory of the development of moral reasoning, paints a very bleak picture of young boys' capacities in this area, with later research finding that girls operate in similar ways (Colby, Gibbs, Lieberman, & Kohlberg, 1983; Walker, 1989). Kohlberg's research, based on earlier more general observations by Piaget, concluded that the development of moral reasoning occurs in three stages: pre-conventional, conventional, and post-conventional. According to Krebs, Denton, and Wark (1997) 'in the Kohlbergian model of morality the moral aspect of personality is defined in terms of the ability to consider the most just solutions to moral dilemmas' (p. 132). Kohlberg's moral stages and levels within these stages are as follows:

Kohlberg's Stages of Moral Development

Pre-conventional
Judgements about right and wrong are made on the basis of physical punishments and the power of those in authority.

Level 1. Punishment and reward orientation. Children make moral decisions based on avoiding punishments or attaining rewards.
Level 2. Instrumental relativism. The needs of others are taken into account, but only if they coincide with the hedonistic needs of the individual making the moral judgement.

Conventional
Judgements are made on the basis of the fixed rules and laws of a society, and a respect for the legitimate authority to enforce those laws.

Level 3. Interpersonal concordance. Moral decisions are based on the desire to please others and in doing so to be a good boy.
Level 4. Law and order. One must show respect for authority by obeying the fixed rules set down by society's lawmakers.

Post-conventional
Judgements are made based on a movement towards individually held moral principles.

Level 5. Social contract. Moral judgements are made based on what is good for society as a whole. Following the law is important, but there is a recognition that laws should have some flexibility and be open to change in order to preserve individual rights.
Level 6. Universal ethic. Moral judgements are made on the basis of deeply held personal beliefs about what is moral which may or may not correspond to the law. Moral decisions are made on the basis of conscience and ethics, defending human rights, and respect for individuals.

Adapted from Tapp and Kohlberg (1971).

The moral reasoning of children in the pre-conventional stage (roughly comparable to those in Piaget's preoperational and concrete operational developmental stages), as one example, is driven by the personal consequences of their actions. Children in this stage make moral decisions based on which actions give them greatest personal advantage, and even when they act in ways which take into account the needs of others, this is not for altruistic reasons, but rather because they see personal advantage in it: 'You scratch my back, and I'll scratch yours.' Kohlberg's view of young children and moral reasoning is that they are driven by self-interest and not particularly concerned about the needs of others. Those in the preconventional stage are 'basically hedonistic' (Tapp & Kohlberg, 1971, p. 69), and solutions to moral dilemmas are just in their eyes when they are to their own advantage. Further, while Piaget felt that children might be able to engage in more flexible types of moral reasoning – shifting between concerns about themselves and concerns about peers – Kohlberg's view was that stages in moral development are more clearly delineated, and the sequence is invariant (Krebs & Denton, 2005). It is interesting to note that in Kohlberg's view the more noble characteristics of acting on higher moral principles are the sole domain of adults, while the more selfish characteristics of acting in self-interest are all that children have available to them.

Questioning the rationalist model of moral development

The adequacy of Kohlberg's work has been challenged by some, including Haidt (2001), Krebs and Denton (2005, 2006), and Krebs et al. (1997). Krebs and Denton challenge the work on the grounds of some of the underlying assumptions of the theory itself. Their research demonstrated a disconnect between the moral decisions people say they would make in a clinical situation, and their actions in real-life situations involving moral reasoning. According to Krebs and Denton (2005)

> In real life, people make moral decisions about themselves and others that matter; the consequences are real. To account for the ways in which people make such decisions, we need an approach that views them as products of social processes and cognitive and affective mechanisms that enable people to achieve their goals and foster their interests in cooperative ways. (p. 647)

Haidt (2001) also questioned Kohlberg's rationalist model, and the assumption that moral reasoning leads to action. Haidt argued that intuition leads to moral action, but after the event this action is often rationalized in terms of reasoning. Importantly, Haidt's basis for action – intuition – is influenced by cultural and social factors, reducing the emphasis on individual reasoning. The idea of acting on intuition was supported by Kohlberg himself who said that some people who reach stage five of moral reasoning can act intuitively within that stage (Kohlberg, 1984). Haidt, however, expanded that idea to all the stages and in doing so provided an opening for the development of a more respectful view of children's capacities and abilities in this area. As an alternative to Kohlberg's estimate of young children and moral reasoning, we can view moral decisions as being based in cultural and social influences. If pre-conventional children behave in seemingly self-centred ways, maybe it is because adults offer children at this age an explicit menu of punishments and rewards for certain behaviour, which undermine their natural capacities to make more altruistic judgements. Instead of assuming that children will behave in self-serving ways, it might be helpful to recall the notion of the disoriented child who, when provided with appropriate reorientation by adults, is capable of acting in ways which benefit others (Rinaldi, 2006). A child who exists in the context of social relationships, (see Chapter 3), is influenced by the society in which he/she lives. Those in these relationships with children, then, have a duty to provide contexts in which children can demonstrate their capacity for altruism. These contexts are those in which a child can feel free to act and behave naturally, without fear of artificial repercussions or punishments. In these environments children can exercise their capacity for making positive moral judgments based on more than simply avoiding negative consequences for themselves, and taking into account the prevailing moral climate in the society in which they live. A respectful view of childhood does not assume that children are naturally driven by self-interest.

Window on Research

Kravtsova (2006) conducted a study in the year 2000 on the responses of 76 Russian children aged 6–9 to stories including questions about values. These responses were compared with the responses of children in a duplicate study originally conducted in 1930. The children were asked to make moral judgements regarding vignettes which were read to them. This study found that children in both time periods believed that the motives for doing certain actions come from a fear of being punished, and also from feelings of sympathy for others. Children in the year 2000, however, felt that feeling sympathy was more important than a fear of being punished compared to the children of the year 1930. The year 2000 children demonstrated a preference for others who are social rather than passive (the opposite was true of the year 1930 children), and when accounting for the actions of the characters in the vignettes the year 2000 children were more likely to refer to their own past experience, or the character's personal characteristics. This study concludes that there were significant differences in what children consider to be morally correct over the time period examined, and that modern Moscow children are more capable of seeing the point of view of others, and therefore are more likely to take into account the community in their decision making rather than acting out of a fear of punishment.

Respecting children's behaviour and morals at home

There has been a long-standing expectation that the home be the main context for the development of good child behaviour and morals. Parents have always been viewed as being the most appropriate source of guidance and discipline in matters relating to behaviour and morals, and have likewise bourn the main brunt of the blame when the actions of children do not meet wider community expectations. As a result, many different means of promoting good behaviour in children, and providing them with a sound set of moral principles on which to guide their actions, have been proposed to, and acted on by, parents. These means range from strictness and corporal punishment, to a more permissive approach in which children behave as they wish, and parents appeal to their better instincts in order to help them to make good decisions.

Corporal punishment:
Shaky logic supporting a risky practice

Corporal punishment at home has been viewed as a useful way of controlling poor behaviour for many years. Data collected by the Global Initiative to End All Corporal Punishment of Children (2007) indicate that corporal punishment in the home is legal in 210 of 231 countries and states worldwide. That 91 per cent of countries allow parents to physically discipline children at home is evidence of the diminished status of children. Some countries that have banned it include such socially conservative states as Romania, the Pitcairn Islands, and Latvia, while other more liberal and wealthy industrialized nations such as the United Kingdom, Australia, the United States, and many European countries continue to allow it. Further, corporal punishment is legal in schools in 122 of the 231 countries and states examined (53 per cent), and also in many penal and alternative care settings for children in these countries, demonstrating the extent to which corporal punishment is accepted.

Corporal punishment for children, however, defies logic. Consider a scenario where a father gives his child a smacking for running down the aisles of a supermarket. This punishment might or might not have been the result of frustration caused by a series of misbehaviours leading up to the incident. Some people would simply not question the right of the father to discipline his child in this way. Indeed, legally, in most countries he has this right. Now consider an alternate scenario where the same man publicly slaps his wife to the point where she cries in pain and humiliation for rushing around a supermarket too quickly. The misbehaviour is essentially the same, as is the punishment. Yet in this scenario most adults would be appalled at the actions of the man, and he may well be criminally charged with assault and spousal abuse, and found guilty and penalized in a court of law. That there is no penalty (and indeed quite the opposite, possible approval) for assaulting a child who is physically weaker, and less able to escape the situation than the wife, makes no sense.

There are other problems with corporal punishment. Research has demonstrated clear links between corporal punishment and child abuse (although it is recognized that the line is blurred with respect to definitions of where corporal punishment ends and child abuse begins). A phone survey of 720 Australian adults found that 45 per cent of those surveyed believed that it was reasonable to leave visible marks on children caused by corporal punishment. Smacking with implements such as canes and belts met with the approval of 10 per cent of those surveyed, and 69 per cent agreed that smacking a naughty child was sometimes necessary (Tucci, Mitchell, & Goddard, 2006). Nobes and Smith (1997) in the United Kingdom found that 91 per cent of children had been hit by their parents, including 75 per cent of babies under 1 year (with 38 per cent being smacked more than once a week). Over 35 per cent of children in this study had experienced severe physical punishment which had the intent, potential, or actually did cause physical and/or psychological harm to the child. The idea of vulnerable children, especially those under one year of age, being treated in this way by adults who are supposed to be loving and nurturing is abhorrent to anyone who believes in preserving the well-being and dignity of children, yet results such as those above are evident in studies in virtually every country in the world. Furthermore, once parents begin physically punishing their children, there is a tendency to increase the severity of such punishments over time as the impact wears off. This escalation has been linked to crossing the line into what is more formally considered to be child abuse (Straus, 1994).

Bandura (1973, 1977, 1986; see also Bandura & Walters, 1959) demonstrated that children learn from observation. He developed his social cognitive theory based on a series of famous experiments he conducted in the 1960s. In these experiments, kindergarten children watched a film of a woman acting aggressively and beating up an inflatable 'Bobo doll' with her body and a hammer while yelling 'socceroo'. Immediately after watching the movie, the children were exposed to a playroom containing a Bobo doll and some hammers. Bandura found that the children imitated the violent behaviour with a high degree of precision, without any encouragement to do so other than having the materials and means available to them. Further experiments involved different variations on the Bobo doll theme, including the beating up of a real clown in a movie. When exposed afterwards to a real clown, the children immediately began to beat up this person. According to Dubanoski, Inaba, and

Gerkewics (1983), those who are physically punished tend to commit violence against other children, teachers, and school property. This is clear evidence of Bandura's theory at work. If this theory is accurate, then it makes sense for children to model the behaviour they see happening to themselves and their siblings at home, producing more violent children where corporal punishment is apparent. Ulman and Straus (2003) found that sons hit their mothers more when the mother was the victim of violence from the father. Further, it is now well-known that children who are victims of abuse are more likely to perpetuate this violent behaviour when they become adults than are children who do not grow up in violent contexts (Saitz, 2006).

Aside from the issues of abuse and appropriateness of physical punishment, there is evidence to suggest that it is largely ineffectual in promoting positive behaviour. Behaviourists such as B. F. Skinner (1953; see also Skinner & Ferster, 1957), in outlining the merits and uses of operant conditioning, listed punishment as the least effectual of all the options available for producing the sorts of behaviours one wants to see in others. Punishment has a tendency to produce the desired results quickly, but these results have a tendency to drop away equally as quickly once the threat of punishment is removed. Skinner recommended the use of positive reinforcement for good behaviour as being the best way to produce lasting change, with this reinforcement having the most significant long-term impact if delivered on a random, or variable ratio schedule. This is why slot machines are so addicting to gamblers; they deliver positive reinforcement (money) on a random basis. Punishment for not putting money in would only result in the avoidance of such machines altogether. Further, Straus (1991) found that corporal punishment, despite having a short-term positive impact on behaviour, is linked to violent behaviour and crime both inside and outside of the family in adulthood. The impact of punishment not only wears off quickly, but may even contribute to this negative adult behaviour.

The impact of over-permissiveness

The other extreme, with children doing as they wish with little guidance or input from parents, is similarly undesirable. While children are inherently good and capable, they do require adult guidance both for ensuring physical safety (as discussed in the previous chapter), and to help them to learn about society's norms, values, and expectations with respect to social behaviour. The chief agents of transmission of these norms, values, and expectations are their parents. It is not so much the nature of the cultural requirements for behaviour of both the child and later adult which are at issue here, but rather the means of transmitting those requirements. And they do need to be transmitted. Children will not be happy if they do not have the ability to engage in positive social interactions with others, and these positive interactions come about as the result of a mutual understanding of the rules for social engagement. Boundaries for behaviour need to be set, and parents are best placed to set those boundaries.

Plenty of evidence exists for not pursuing a permissive approach to parenting. Sandstrom (2007) found a relationship between permissive mothering and relational aggression. Rutledge et al. (2007) found a positive correlation between child obesity and permissive parenting. Gonzalez and Wolters (2006) found a relationship between permissive parenting and decreased achievement motivation in children in academic work, specifically mathematics. Morrongiello, Corbett, Lasenby, Johnston, and McCourt (2006) found that permissive parents used strategies to teach about safety in the home which actually elevated the risk of children becoming injured. Permissive parenting does not provide children with the structure that they need to develop their own ideas about what is right and what is wrong, and how to self-monitor and best ensure that their behaviour is socially acceptable. Consider the example of the 4-year-old child who becomes angry while playing a game and tells his father he hates him. The permissive father might say 'That hurts Daddy's feelings' but nonetheless allow the behaviour to continue unchecked, with the rationale being that it is healthy for a child to be able to express his emotions (even if they are negative). It is healthy to express emotions, but few would agree that this is an appropriate way to do so. Tolerating such behaviour ignores the fact that telling a parent they are hated (even if done so in a moment of anger) is socially unacceptable, rude, and hurtful. In this circumstance the child learns nothing about where the boundaries of acceptable and unacceptable behaviour lie, or about the need to keep certain behaviours in check because they have an impact on others. The permissive parent in this circumstance does the child a disservice because he does not teach the child the difference between right and wrong.

The authoritative parent

An approach which has some merit, and which certainly respects a child's inherent goodness and competence in controlling their own behaviour, and developing morals, lies in authoritative parenting. Authoritative parenting is not to be confused with authoritarian parenting. Authoritarian parenting is akin to a dictatorship, where parents set all the rules and expect strict adherence to those rules, enforcing them through their physical and psychological power. Authoritative parenting can be viewed more as a mentorship, albeit a close and loving one. An authoritative parent is a guide and positive example to their children, one with a deep relationship and bond to those children. One who suggests and negotiates the right course of action, but who is nonetheless willing to set boundaries as required. An authoritative parent leads children willingly towards desirable behaviour through their own personal credibility as loving, caring, and knowledgeable parent. As an example, where an authoritarian parent will set a child's bedtime and enforce lights out rigidly, an authoritative parent might be more willing to negotiate a bedtime routine, providing this negotiation takes place within commonly understood boundaries. For example, moving bedtime from 8:00 p.m. to midnight might be unacceptable to the authoritative parent (who would explain why this is so to the child), but perhaps an extra hour delay in the bedtime might be acceptable providing the time was spent reading quietly in bed. This could be negotiated with the child. Milevsky, Schlechter, Netter, and Keehn (2007) found that authoritative parenting was more likely to produce adolescents with higher self-esteem, less depression, and greater life satisfaction compared with those who grew up under a more permissive home environment. The middle ground that being an authoritative parent provides between permissiveness and authoritarianism might be a desirable and respectful way to work with children, and one which might well have positive effects for the entire family.

Window on Research

Steinberg, Blatt-Eisengart, and Cauffman (2006) conducted a study on parenting style (authoritative, authoritarian, indulgent, and neglectful) and adolescent adjustment involving a sample of 1,355 adolescents aged 14–18 years old who had committed serious juvenile criminal offences. Most of the children in the sample were poor, from single-parent homes with poorly educated parents, and were from lower socio-economic urban neighbourhoods in the United States. The majority were from racial and ethnic minority groups. This population was chosen for the study primarily because the links between parenting style and adolescent adjustment have not been adequately studied in populations at greatest risk for problematic development. One of the purposes of the study was to see if authoritative parenting had the same positive impact on psychosocial competence, school success, and the internalization or externalization of problems with this high risk population as it does with other populations.

The initial data were gathered using interviews with the adolescents, a parental warmth scale, and a parental firmness scale. On the basis of the data, families were divided into the four groups of authoritative ($N = 184$), authoritarian ($N = 104$), neglectful ($N = 173$), and indulgent ($N = 100$). The results showed that authoritative parenting was lower among white families, and that younger adolescents were more likely to characterize their parents as authoritative than were older adolescents. Other measures were used to determine school success, psychosocial competence, and the internalization or externalization of problems.

Steinberg et al. (2006) found higher levels of psychosocial maturity and school success, and lower levels of internalizing distress and externalizing problems in children from authoritative backgrounds than those from other backgrounds. Those from neglectful backgrounds were found to have the lowest levels of maturity, school success, and be more prone to internalization of distress and externalization of problems than all other groups. Those from indulgent or authoritarian backgrounds were placed between these two extremes. These findings were consistent with studies conducted on other, lower risk populations of adolescents and children, and supports the effectiveness of the adoption of authoritative parenting styles across a wide range of socio-economic contexts.

Respecting children's behaviour and morals at school

For pre-service and new teachers, behaviour management in the classroom is one of the most daunting tasks they face (McNally, I'anson, Whewell, & Wilson, 2005). Pre-service teachers are rightly taught that children cannot learn in chaos, and that it is their job to ensure that children behave appropriately while at school. This responsibility is even enshrined in most legislation and policy relating to the responsibilities of a teacher. McNally et al. observe that

> there is no shortage of anecdotal evidence from students on or returning from field placements: 'welcome to the wild west' and 'you are now entering the war zone' are examples of the early greetings voiced to students often, it has to be said, with some humour. (p. 170)

Behind every good joke, though, there is an element of truth. Teachers are burdened with the expectation that they must control the behaviour of the children they teach. This is a stressful proposition. It is all well and good when children cooperate and the techniques for controlling behaviour work, but what occurs when children are uncooperative and do not respond to the teacher's requests for good behaviour? The need to effectively control the behaviour of children weighs heavily in these circumstances and is stressful to teachers. Roffey (2004) says that 20 per cent of teachers leave the profession within 3 years of graduation from university, and 50 per cent leave within 5 years, often citing student behaviour as the primary reason for their departure. While those who remain long enough to become experienced teachers cite student behaviour as becoming less of a problem over time, it is never entirely eliminated as an issue (McNally et al., 2005).

Welcome to your new class . . . now control those kids!

The primary source of stress in this area might be that teachers are required to control the behaviour of another. Is this a reasonable or even possible expectation? This expectation sets teachers and students up for an adversarial relationship ('welcome to the war zone'), or one which is founded on the teacher being the absolute authority and final word. Teachers are provided with strategies and structures which enable them in most cases to maintain an environment where children generally do as the teacher asks. These strategies and structures have fallen under the banner of what are known as classroom management techniques, and are generally based on the use of a teacher's power as legitimized by the school and members of society. Where this management style is adopted (and, while common in varying degrees, it must be acknowledged that not all teachers and schools operate in this way), the teacher in collusion with the school directs where students sit, what types of communication they may participate in, when they can eat, drink, and use the bathroom, what clothing they can wear (dress codes and uniforms), and what activities they can participate in. Classes transit through the school in two quiet lines. They must keep the noise level down in the gym. They must sit on the floor for stories and instructions. They may not speak without raising their hand. They may not criticize. They must not waste time in class. In short, they must obey the teacher at all times, and ensure that they do not contravene any of the school or classroom rules which have usually been set by adults. The teacher maintains professional distance and distributes rewards and punishments as he or she sees fit. Not all teachers who manage behaviour in their classroom demand absolute compliance from all children all the time, but their position of authority in the school implicitly or explicitly sends a message to children that they could implement more totalitarian measures if behaviour does not remain good. Consider the oft-heard threat that 'if the noise continues at this level then we will be working in absolute silence for the rest of the class'. This way of working is not the fault of the teacher in most cases; it is the result of the requirement for them to control the behaviour of children.

Behaviourist approaches to classroom management: Putting out fires

The vast majority of the techniques teachers are provided with to effectively manage the classroom are behaviourist in nature. Behaviourism in and of itself is not necessarily a bad thing. Indeed, even social constructivist theorist Vygotsky conceded that behaviourism is the basis for nearly all our action and learning (DeVries, 2000). But behaviourist techniques are supposed to produce a more or less automatic response; one which the subject does not really have to think about. Thinking is for cognitivists, and Skinner himself was not terribly concerned with the thought process behind producing a desired behaviour, just that the behaviour itself was produced on cue (Skinner, 1987). However, a heavy reliance on behavioural techniques for classroom management purposes removes the expectation that children will consider their actions and the impact they might have on themselves or others. Instead, in extreme circumstances, children will only behave in certain ways in order to get a reward, or to avoid an undesirable circumstance or punishment. Consider the following common techniques for promoting good behaviour and their links to behaviourism:

1. A child is rewarded with a sticker for working quietly in his desk for the entire class. A behaviourist would say that this is a good strategy for having the child repeat the behaviour. Especially if stickers come according to a variable ratio, working quietly at the desk will become habit, and the stickers can be gradually withdrawn (faded) leaving only the desirable behaviour.

2. A child spends recess indoors and is only allowed to go outside once she has completed all her work from the previous class. Behaviourists call this negative reinforcement. The child behaves in a certain way (completing work) in order to gain relief from an unpleasant situation. Eventually, the child will learn to complete her work in class so as to avoid the unpleasantness of recess indoors.

3. A child contravenes school rules by swearing at the teacher. He is punished by being sent to the principal's office where he will be scolded and made to apologise to his teacher following a period of time-out. Behaviourists view punishment as the least effective of all strategies, but still advocate for its effectiveness in situations where a consequence must be implemented. If the child dislikes the punishment he will, at least in the short term, discontinue the behaviour.

In each of the above instances the behaviour of child is being manipulated by a schedule of rewards and punishments of an extrinsic nature. The will of the child is subjugated to the authority of the teacher, the school rules, and the sorts of rewards and punishments it is within their authority to administer. The locus of control is external. In the first example, the child does not learn the potential value of working quietly during some parts of the day, only that rewards come to those who comply with this demand. In the second example, the child does not get the opportunity to consider the value of completing work during class time, only that it needs to get finished if recess is to be spent outside. In the third example, the child does not change his actions on the basis of reflection on how his teacher may feel, but rather changes because being sent to the principal's office is unnerving and time-out is dull. Children might behave better in the classroom as a result of these measures, but the reality is that it teaches them very little about general principles of conduct which can transfer to appropriate behaviour in a variety of contexts. The child may learn not to swear at his teacher, but learning that may have no impact on his swearing at his soccer coach.

Developing self-discipline

Alternatives exist. They are certainly more complex and harder to implement than behaviourist techniques, but they are proactive and better preserve the dignity of the child. Good alternatives help children to develop internal loci of control; rewards for good behaviour take on an intrinsic aspect. This, it could be argued, has greater potential for generalization of positive behaviour across contexts and situations, and may have a more positive long-term impact.

First, the nature of what constitutes poor behaviour needs to be reconsidered. Poor behaviour is a socially constructed concept; adults decide what sort of behaviour is acceptable or not, and it varies from context to context. In western society, asking questions of the teacher is generally considered to be positive; evidence that the child is interested in learning about the topic. However, in some cultures this same behaviour is akin to calling the teacher incompetent, or questioning his or her authority, and so is regarded as rude. Some teachers get so caught up in running an efficient classroom that they lose sight of which behaviours are important to discourage in order to maintain a safe and effective learning environment. According to experienced educator and school administrator Dean Caouette, some teachers regard every breach of the rules, however small, as a personal affront because they expect all children to obey the rules all of the time. In Caouette's view, a more positive approach would be to acknowledge that children will misbehave at times, and to judge each infraction of the rules according to its merits, while also actively teaching children what the expectation is rather than assuming that they have learned this by osmosis (Personal communication, 26 October 2007). This offers teachers some much-needed flexibility. Teachers need to seriously consider how they use their power, and examine if some of their expectations regarding behaviour really improve student safety and learning. For example, does the wearing of a hat in the classroom represent a serious threat to student learning and overall discipline? Does getting a drink without permission undermine the effectiveness of the classroom learning environment? The answer to these questions will depend on the context in which a teacher operates, but the point is that many of the past assumptions about what is and what is not appropriate classroom behaviour need to be re-examined in terms of their relevance to individual classroom and school contexts.

Secondly, in order to offer children greater dignity it is desirable to get away from the view that classrooms are places where children need to be managed. Rather, classrooms should be places where relationships are built. Children with strong relationships with their teacher and peers are less likely to misbehave (Albert, 2003; Wong & Wong, 1998). There is a tendency to isolate and remove children with behaviour difficulties from the classroom situation either sporadically or permanently, resulting in children who become alienated and more problematic than ever. A better approach might lie in doing the exact opposite: building a community around these children based on positive relationships and interdependence (Peterson & Loreman, 2005). This is certainly difficult, and we do not yet have all the answers on how to effectively do this with children who, for example, frequently exhibit violent behaviour. For now, the best that can be said is that teachers wanting to employ a relationship-based approach to classroom management in challenging situations need to call on support from their entire school community, including children, parents, colleagues, and support staff in order to solve problems as they occur in a contextually relevant way. Children who are connected to their classroom and who are not alienated are much more likely to be engaged, and to make positive contributions to the classroom climate.

In the same way that authoritative parenting has value for respecting children's behaviour while at the same time providing the guidance they need, authoritative teaching has value. An authoritative teacher is not a child's friend, but neither are they a distant, objective professional. Teaching is not a clinical enterprise, and as such a clinical approach is not called for. An authoritative teacher is one who shows children that they are warm, caring, and interested in pursuing a relationship with them, while at the same time retaining the power to make decisions that need to be made and to run the classroom in an efficient manner. An authoritative teacher encourages respect between children, and children and adults, while avoiding the implementation of systems of punitive rewards and punishments wherever possible. Teachers do not need to resort to using the formal power they have, but can rather lead based on the influence they will have once children know they are excellent instructors who make good decisions, and who care about them and like them. Consider the following examples of the establishment of classroom rules. An authoritarian teacher would simply set the rules and expect full compliance, while a permissive teacher would set no rules and allow children to guess what is acceptable and what is not according to the circumstance. Neither of these two examples adequately respects children's ability to set limits on their own behaviour in concert with guidance from a responsible adult. In contrast, near the beginning of the year the authoritative teacher might hold a class meeting to discuss what the rules for the year might be. The children would suggest possible rules, and the teacher would lead a discussion on the merits (or otherwise) of the various suggestions, vetoing unacceptable suggestions along the way if necessary (and explaining the rationale behind the veto). The entire class would then vote on which rules are retained, but in order to get to this point the teacher has already essentially approved each option by not exercising a veto, and has influenced the outcome during the discussion of the merits of each proposed rule. The teacher can live with the decision made, and the children more likely to comply with rules they had a hand in devising, resulting in a more proactive approach to promoting good behaviour. This empowers both the teacher and the children to work together in establishing and maintaining a positive classroom environment.

This chapter has examined some of the negative views various elements of society hold regarding children's behaviour and morals, and has suggested some positive alternatives to these views and practices when working with children. Children are not as simplistic in this area as many people suggest, and in fact are capable of making good decisions, of cooperating with others, and of taking the needs and feelings of others into account when acting. Children need mentors and guides rather than authoritarian approaches and management practices in order to best demonstrate their inherent competence in this area.

Case Study: The Behaviour School

I taught for 2 years in a school for teenagers who had been removed from their secondary schools because of a violent act, or a series of violent acts, they had committed. These children were invariably years behind their grade level with respect to curriculum expectations, had difficulty concentrating, were usually quick to anger, and prone to violent outbursts against their peers and school staff, including myself. These students were considered to be uncontrollable and too dangerous to attend regular schools, even in special segregated classrooms. Violence in some form was a daily feature of life at this school. At any one time there were between 15 and 20 students in the school, divided into three classes of between 5 and 7 students taught by a teacher and a teacher assistant. The philosophy behind the establishment of this school was not so much that these students would be rehabilitated, but rather that students at other schools would be protected from them. Occasionally students were thought to be ready to return to a regular school, but this was extremely rare and was never successful in the 2 years I was at the school. The building was ill-suited for its purpose, being formerly a home for unwed mothers in the 1950s. My classroom was a 10 metre by 5 metre rectangular space, the result of a wall being knocked out between two bedrooms. The space was a problem, children with antisocial tendencies confined in close quarters with a teacher and an assistant was a recipe for disaster.

The students spent the morning on academics and the afternoon involved in physical education and recreational pursuits. During academic work little social interaction was encouraged as fights were too common. The students completed individual work in as isolated an environment as possible. How much they completed varied. Putting too much pressure on these students to complete work resulted in violence. Instead, a system whereby students would earn points for completed work was instituted. A set number of points was awarded for good behaviour and completed work. At the end of the day these points could be used to purchase a reward (usually chewing gum), and at the end of the week those with enough accumulated points got the weekly reward which was usually watching a movie, playing pool, or some other enjoyable activity. This system worked well as long as students earned points. Those who for some reason did not earn enough points often resorted to violent tantrums.

- What was the value in the behaviour school for the students who attended?
- What do you think of the points system used to promote good behaviour and work completion? Given the population, what other realistic options might have existed?
- What alternatives to the behaviour school exist?

Discussion Questions

- Divide a page into three columns. At the top of each column write Authoritarian, Authoritative and Permissive. Outline the key features of each approach for parents. What does parenting look like in each category? Repeat the activity for teachers.
- In your opinion, what school rules are required to enhance learning, and what sorts of rules commonly in schools serve no real purpose in enhancing learning or promoting positive behaviour?
- Reflect on some of the stories your parents and grandparents told you about their behaviour, or the behaviour of other children, when they were young. How was this behaviour different or similar to what you see today?

Further Resources

Albert, L. (2003). *Cooperative discipline* (Rev. edn). USA: Ags.

Global Initiative to End All Corporal Punishment of Children website: www. endcorporalpunishment.org

Jeanne Ballantine on authoritative parenting: www.findarticles.com/p/articles/ mi_qa3614/is_200110/ai_n8958286

Respecting Children's Differences

6

Chapter Outline

Introduction

This chapter discusses some of the broad differences seen in children, including disability, social, racial, ethnic, religious, sexual orientation, and gender group. Despite the large differences between these groups, each faces common challenges of discrimination and prejudice. In western society some of this discrimination and prejudice is to varying degrees subtle, but nonetheless exists even where an exterior veneer of inclusiveness is apparent.

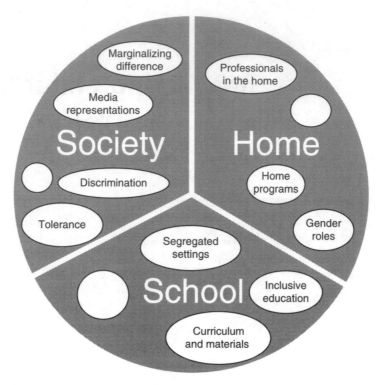

Figure 6.1 Chapter outline figure

The big picture

One might marvel at the level of acceptance, adaptations, and concessions made in virtually all areas of society in order to help level the playing field for children with individual differences. There are special classes, and in some cases special schools, for children whose differences range from disability to gender to religion and/or cultural background. Special provisions in sporting clubs and organizations such as the Scouting Movement exist to enable the participation of children who are different. Children from a variety of minority backgrounds frequently feature in media touting their achievements and contributions to society.

Scratch beneath the surface, though, and these seemingly positive developments have a dark side, and in many respects are deliberately designed to further marginalize those who already live outside of the mainstream. Take the above-mentioned Scouting Movement, for example. The policy of Scout Associations throughout the world is to involve and include children with disabilities. Despite this, however, their unwillingness to truly support children with disabilities to fully participate in activities in some countries is evident. The South African Scout Association (2003) makes this explicit in their brochure of advice to Scouting groups on the issue of including children with disabilities. On the surface they seem to encourage inclusion, but then add a number of major caveats, stating:

> The would-be Cub/Scout should be physically fit enough to get about with the other Cubs or Scouts. He or she should be clean in his habits and able to feed himself or herself. The mentally disabled Scout should be able to attend to their personal needs, and to obey all simple instructions and understand enough to be able to enter into Cub/ Scout games and simple ceremonies. . . . It is essential to give the backward Cub or Scout the most careful patient and unobtrusive enquiry and thought. . . . The child should fit into the programs and not the programs fitted around the child. (pp. 3–4)

This brochure clearly encourages exclusionary admission practices. If they are admitted, children must fit in because the advice is that programmes will not be adapted to meet the needs of a particular child. On the surface this organization seems to embrace all children, but a closer look at the above statement reveals that the opposite is true.

The disguise of tolerance

The Scout Movement is perhaps a soft target given the primarily volunteer-run nature of the organization. To be fair, they are by no means alone in their approach to working with children who are different, and are just one example of a more widespread problem. Under the guise of protecting the secularity of government-run institutions (specifically schools), effective from 2 September 2004, the French government banned the wearing of Islamic headscarves (part of the Islamic hijab, or modesty) in public schools (National Assembly and Senate of France, 2004). In the wake of post-9/11 global religious tensions, this was widely seen as religious discrimination, and had the added aspect of gender discrimination as it is only girls who wear such headscarves. The law also, however, discriminated against symbols from any religious group including, for example, Sikh turbans, Jewish skull-caps, and large Christian crosses (n.a., 2004a). The implication of this law was that any child from a family who felt unable to remove such articles for religious reasons was then excluded from French public schools. The unevenness with which certain groups were targeted was evident. For example, there is no religious directive for Christian children to wear visible crosses, however, those from Islamic backgrounds who wear the headscarf do so because in their personal circumstance they believe it to be a necessary prerequisite for following their faith. Indeed, in October 2004 a number of French schoolgirls were expelled from school for refusing to remove their scarves (n.a., 2004b); ironically despite protestations from the French President of the time, Jacques Chirac, that France was in fact demonstrating its tolerance for all religions in protecting the secular nature of its institutions, and therefore not promoting one religion at the expense of another.

Many organizations provide lip-service and advocate a tolerant attitude towards difference, yet are unwilling to change much in terms of the accommodations they make. This is part of the problem with tolerance. The word tolerance is used by many as a means of discussing how well they accept diversity: to be tolerant is good. To merely tolerate each other's differences, however, is reminiscent of an awful party where guests put up with a host's obnoxious behaviour for a couple of hours in order to be polite before making excuses and leaving. Tolerance, therefore, is a good start but is not to be equated with acceptance; true acceptance of difference is what should be aspired to. Acceptance means more than simply allowing a child to join an organization or attend a school and then expecting them to fit in. Acceptance of diversity means to recognize value in the difference, while at the same time emphasising that all children share in a common humanity and need to be able to participate in all facets of society together. In the above example of Scouting, for instance, the programme should be designed to fit the child. It should fit all children, so that no child is disadvantaged or left out. Girls wearing Islamic headscarves should not only be allowed to do so, but their cultural and religious background should be celebrated for enriching the broader society in which they live.

The power of media stereotypes

Throughout this book mention has been made of the media's contribution to many of the negative ways in which children are viewed, but nowhere is this contribution more evident than in the area of individual difference. The western media has been accused of racism, sexism, political conservatism (consider the Murdoch media empire), and condescension towards people with disabilities (Bradley, 1995; Campbell, 1995; Johnson, 2007; LeBesco, 2006). Media frequently and deliberately use out-dated terminology such as 'handicapped' or 'disabled child' (as opposed to the more acceptable person-first language of 'child with a disability') which sends a blunt message that this disability is the main and defining feature of that child. The disability takes precedence over the fact that he/she is a child, and it is used in order to accentuate their difference and perpetuate their marginalization. The same can be said of phrases like 'poor children', 'Muslim children', or 'black children'. According to Haller, Dorries, and Rahn (2006) 'even something as mundane as the words used to refer to a group are important because they have ramifications for both the self-perception of people with disabilities and what the general public believes about disability' (p. 62). In the case of children with disabilities, this is done to link them even more strongly to the condescending and clichéd message of courage which often follows. Hear the words 'disabled child' in the media and one can be near certain that a heart-warming tale of courage against the odds is not far behind. Disability is feared by many, and some even feel guilty for being able-bodied when around people with disabilities (Loreman et al., 2005). To promote children with disabilities as heroes, then, helps to alleviate some of that fear and guilt. Kama (2004) identified two broad types of media representations of people with disabilities. Kama argues that existing media representations are the result of a tradition of viewing disability as being a medical calamity in need of remedy. Because of this, people with disabilities are represented on the one hand as objects of pity. On the other hand disability is seen in terms of being created by members of society, and those with disabilities who manage to overcome barriers are seen as heroic. Kama calls these two broad media representations of people with disabilities the 'pitiful handicapped' and the 'supercrip'. Both representations serve to place people with disabilities outside of mainstream society. Even the case of the 'supercrip' needs to be recognized in terms of how condescending the image is. According to Wall (1987)

> The late Lew Hankins, director of United Cerebral Palsy and a man who had spent most of his life in a wheelchair, once told me that he often had people tell him how 'amazing' he was. He noted that a disability is not something you sign up for to prove how 'brave' you are. Rather, it is a fact of life and you try to give it as little importance as possible. (p. 237)

Girls, too, suffer from images in the media which emphasize unflattering gender stereotypes. Consider movies such as 'Million Dollar Baby' where a young woman is portrayed in a heroic role similar to the above simply for competing in what is a traditionally male sport; the goals attained are the result of efforts so notable it becomes the subject of a (albeit fictional) movie. Much attention has recently been devoted to Danica Patrick for being the first woman to win an Indy car race, the 2008 Indy Japan 300. Her sporting achievement has been overshadowed by media coverage focusing on the fact that she is a woman succeeding in a traditionally male sport, and a photogenic one at that. Even her official website promotes this aspect, featuring pop music and a large, flattering photo of Patrick, notably without a car in sight (see www.danicaracing.com). A young woman winning an Indy car race is seen as a novelty rather than something that might be expected, and is reduced to the status of a 'pin-up' girl. Girls watching movies such as the above and paying attention to such media coverage might well be led to believe that playing sport is an extraordinary achievement in and of itself, and even amusing, rather than being simply normal as is the case for many boys. In this way, and through a myriad of other media representations, girls are marginalized and assigned to roles which are more limited than those available to boys. Daniels and Leaper (2006) found that women athletes are largely invisible in mainstream magazines teen girls read, reinforcing how marginalized girls are in this particular area. Further, where they are visible, it is often in ways similar to Danica Patrick, where they are presented in overtly sexual ways rather than in ways celebrating their sporting achievements. For example, the Australian National Women's Soccer Team (the Matildas) released a fundraising calendar ahead of the 2000 Olympics featuring naked photographs of the team. The 'Women of Sports' website (www.sports-wired.com/women) features hundreds of similar pictures of women athletes ranging from a variety of Olympians to golfers, tennis players, and other professional team and individual sports women.

Anyone doubting this limiting of roles for girls need only watch a short amount of children's television. Advertisements generally consist of boys charging around shooting each other with water pistols, while the alternative for girls is to wear pretty bracelets or brush the hair of toy ponies. The message is that boys are physical and tough, while girls are pretty and sweet, and that these differences are important. Furnham, Abramsky, and Gunter (1997), in an analysis of British and American children's advertising, found that males were more numerous in the advertisements, and also that they generally occupied more central and authoritative positions. This would seem to reinforce the view that girls are on the margins, and that according to the media this is the natural order of society.

Discrimination

One purpose of representing children from minority and gender groups in this manner is to make it easier to discriminate against them. In order to be enacted, discrimination requires two elements: prejudice and power (Link & Phelan, 2001). Without some form of prejudice one would not be compelled to discriminate against a group, and without power one would not be able to. When it comes to children with individual and group differences, there is no shortage of both prejudice and power in society to make discrimination a reality. It is perhaps an uncomfortable truth that people who are not from minority groups often benefit from discrimination in some way, even if they are not active participants. For example, children without disabilities might not have to compete with children who have disabilities for places in some schools because the children with disabilities in the region may have been pushed to attend special schools. The child without the disability did not actively discriminate, yet still derived benefit from the actions of those who did. The following discrimination matrix (Table 6.3) highlights what sort of discrimination occurs when certain types of discrimination are employed by various types of participants in society.

The following criteria apply to the descriptors used in the discrimination matrix in Table 6.3:

Table 6.1 Participants in discrimination

Engaged Affirmative
Someone who is highly aware of discrimination, and actively works to see it eliminated where it already exists, and not instituted in areas where it does not exist. This can be for personal advantage, or on the basis of working in support of a moral principle.

Ignorant
Someone who is unaware of the existence of discrimination in the various contexts. For example, a young child who has never encountered discriminatory attitudes or environments. Alternatively, an adult who does not realize that certain practices are either discriminatory or enabling.

Passive
Someone who is aware of the existence of discrimination but is not inclined to change their attitudes or practices in order to stop it. Will not discriminate if given an easy choice, but also will not forgo discrimination if it takes any effort. May remain passive out of fear, intimidation, or for personal gain.

Engaged Negative
Someone who is not only aware of discrimination, but actively works to see it maintained where it already exists, and instituted in areas where it does not exist. This is usually for personal advantage.

Table 6.2 Categories of discrimination

Positive
Children from minority groups are given advantages not available to those in the mainstream. This form of discrimination is extremely rare, but for example may occur in organizations such as school systems trying to ensure that they do not discriminate by reserving spaces for the inclusion of children from minority groups.

None
There is no disadvantage to a child from a minority group. These are generally termed enabling environments where all children can participate in all activities.

Latent
Structures which exist in society which may not be obvious but which still result in discrimination. For example, low representation of people from particular cultural groups involved in teacher preparation programmes at universities means that teachers may not leave university with enabling attitudes, and therefore may pass this on to the children they teach once they start teaching.

Harmful
Children being denied club or association membership, school entry, access to community events and so on, on the basis of their individual difference. This is the commonly understood view of discrimination.

Discrimination in some form will almost always exist for minority social groups, however people who respect children with differences will always work towards the ideal of having engaged affirmative adults and children working to preserve contexts where no discrimination exists, or occasionally where positive discrimination is enacted as required (e.g. retaining places in regular schools so that children from minority backgrounds are fairly represented).

Table 6.3 Discrimination Matrix

Participants in discrimination	Type of discrimination			
	Positive	None	Latent	Harmful
Engaged affirmative	Works to promote some advantages for children from minority groups over the mainstream. May try and enlist the support of ignorant and passive participants.	Works to preserve current context, and in extreme cases may even seek extra privileges for those from minority groups.	Points out latent forms of discrimination in society and will try and engage ignorant and passive participants' support. Often works to remove discrimination through awareness and negotiation.	Will try and engage ignorant and passive participants' support. Will work to eliminate existing discriminatory structures, and to protest and stop new discriminatory barriers and practices.
Ignorant	Positive discrimination continues unchecked. If ignorant participants become aware of the positive discrimination they may be inclined to either stop or support it.	Full inclusion. For example, a child who is ignorant of discriminatory attitudes interacting in a non-discriminatory environment will accept others' differences.	Discrimination in society continues unchecked. If ignorant participants become aware of the latent discrimination they may be inclined to either stop or support it.	Discrimination accelerates because active participants accept ignorance as acquiescence for actions. Ignorant people in actively harmful discriminatory environments are more likely to be negatively influenced as they see no wrong in the actions.
Passive	The passive participant will support positive discriminatory structures by maintaining involvement in institutions and the like that discriminate positively, providing it is convenient to them.	'Sink or swim' mentality for children from minority groups. Passive participants in non-discriminatory environments may not work against inclusion, but neither will they assist with it.	The passive participant will support society's discriminatory structures by maintaining involvement in institutions and the like that discriminate providing it is convenient to them.	Lends tacit support to discriminatory practices. They may not tell the offensive joke, but will certainly laugh at it!
Engaged negative	Will try and engage ignorant and passive participants' support. Will work to eliminate existing positive discriminatory structures, and to protest and stop new positive discriminatory policies and practices.	The active participant will engage in no discrimination if they lack the power to act on their prejudices.	Will try and engage ignorant and passive participants' support. Will work to maintain existing discriminatory structures.	Will try and engage ignorant and passive participants' support. Will work to maintain existing discriminatory structures, and to construct new discriminatory barriers and practices.

Window on Research

Ritchey and Fishbein (2001) conducted a study to determine the extent to which friends influence the prejudice and stereotypes of white adolescents. A total of 426 male (*N* = 164) and female (*N* = 272) students in Grades 9 and 11 completed a survey that evaluated race, homosexual, gender, HIV/AIDS, and fat prejudice. A statistical procedure known as regression analysis, which examines whether responses on one scale impact responses on another scale, was used. The procedure compared the above survey of 'intolerance' with a set of questions which helped to evaluate if the influence of friends was conditional on friendship reciprocity, closeness, number of friends, parenting style, congruity of friends' prejudices and the degree of prejudice indicated by the teen completing the survey. No association was found between friends' prejudices and stereotypes, meaning that in this study the views of friends had no impact on the prejudices and stereotypes of individuals. In the words of Ritchey and Fishbein 'In the realm of prejudice and stereotyping, adolescent birds of a feather do *not* flock together' (p. 199). Ritchey and Fishbein explained this by arguing that topics such as this are infrequently discussed by adolescents, who in any case attend schools with homogeneous populations, and assume that their friends hold views similar to their own. Also, they argued that although teens might engage in behaviour which might be considered to be intolerant in situations involving peer pressure, their actual views and beliefs might be quite different, and given the results of the study are formed outside of the sphere of peer influence.

Respecting children's differences at home

Home is often a safe haven for children from diverse backgrounds; it is a place where they can generally engage in their religious and cultural practices with the full support and often participation of their families. While outside institutions may discriminate, the family usually governs what happens in the home. Notwithstanding the possibility of discrimination from within the family, in that environment to an extent the discrimination evident in broader society is ameliorated. This, however, is often not the case for two specific groups where society imposes itself on family life to an extent which is generally greater than is the case with other groups. These groups are children with disabilities, and gender groups.

Disability and home institutionalization

The vast majority of children with disabilities are raised in the family home, perhaps with the exception of some extreme cases which preclude this for reasons such as medical necessity. This situation is ideal in terms of respecting the child; children should be raised in the family home wherever possible. What becomes problematic, though, is the need for medical or therapeutic interventions which often accompany the life of a child with a disability. A colleague of mine, himself the father of a large family including a now-adult daughter with a severe and multiple disability, remarked how he and his wife chose not to institutionalize his daughter. Instead, he said, 'our home became the institution'. Such was the need for medical and therapeutic intervention that his family for years had to schedule their lives around his daughter's appointments and needs. This is not to say that the home was not the best environment for this girl to grow up in, or that the parents and siblings would have wanted it any other way, just that the impact it had on the family needs to be considered. What was problematic in this instance, and can be problematic in many other cases, is the necessarily intrusive nature of home-based community care and intervention. Families of children with disabilities are often faced with a procession of professionals on high rotation both in the early intervention years, and later while at school. Parenting children with disabilities is associated with higher than usual levels of stress in the parents (Esdaile & Greenwood, 2003), and the need to maintain a rigid schedule based on the availability of professionals can contribute to this, even though the positive outcomes of the interventions are thought to outweigh the negative impacts of the demands (Trudgeon & Carr, 2007). The same can be said of professionals working with immigrant families whose first language is different from the region in which they now live. Home programmes to promote the learning of the new language can become intrusive. Professionals working with families, then, need to be sensitive to this, and administrators of programmes need to allow for flexibility in scheduling to ensure that the family can engage in at least some of the normal spontaneous activities people engage in. Regular Wednesday morning appointments may not work well for everyone, and professionals should resist the temptation to judge or become frustrated when families request flexibility.

It is not just the scheduling of professional visits that creates tension within the homes of children with disabilities (and, indeed, those from different language backgrounds), but sometimes it is the expectations professionals place on families in terms of delivering programmes in the home that causes difficulties. Johnson and Hastings (2002), in their UK study of parents of children with autism, found that many parents cited a lack of time and energy as being a barrier to implementing home-based early behavioural intervention programmes (see also Hastings & Johnson, 2001). Further, Schwichtenberg and Poehlmann (2007) found that parents of children with autism who participated in home Applied Behavioural Analysis programmes experienced elevated depressive symptoms, and the level of intensity of the programme was related to maternal depression and personal strain. Certainly pressure from having to implement home-based programmes is not limited to parents of children with autism, and it is probable that the results from studies such as these can be generalized to almost any type of inflexible home-based programme.

The problem of family stress related to home-based programmes for children with disabilities, where it exists, might in part be due to conflicting ideas between the parents and professionals regarding programme implementation. The clinical background of many therapists (including occupational therapists, speech-language pathologists, psychologists, physical therapists, nurses and doctors) has resulted in specific ways of working. Disability is medicalized, and treatments and programmes are prescribed (in some countries, such as Ukraine, special professionals known as defectologists coordinate such interventions). Therapists and medical staff work from a model where programmes and treatments are devised and delivered, and their outcomes are assessed (Loreman et al., 2005). This model is sometimes at odds with what parents are able and willing to do in the home. In situations where parents are not meeting programme demands, conflict can occur. Professionals might be frustrated that the parents are not adhering to the programme and that outcomes are not being met, and the parents might be frustrated by the possible expectation that family time would be spent in therapy situations. Often these situations can be resolved if there is sensitivity and flexibility on both sides, but if adjustments need to be made by one side only, then that party should be the professional. Parents need to be the bottom line. They are the ones who will in most cases be making decisions which they think are in the best interests of their child throughout their childhood (and possibly beyond), and professionals need to respect these decisions. If family time watching a movie occasionally takes precedence over working on certain therapeutic goals, then so be it. In the vast majority of cases nobody has a better perspective on what is best for their child than the parents.

Reinforcing gender stereotypes at home

While issues regarding respect for the differences of children with disabilities in the home have a tendency to come from pressures outside of the home, issues regarding the promotion of gender stereotypes tend to begin from an early age as a result of interactions in the home. According to Witt (1997)

> children regularly learn to adopt gender roles which are not always fair to both sexes. As children move through childhood and into adolescence, they are exposed to many factors which influence their attitudes and behaviours regarding gender roles. These attitudes and behaviours are generally learned first in the home and are then reinforced by the child's peers, school experience, and television viewing. However, the strongest influence on gender role development seems to occur within the family setting, with parents passing on, both overtly and covertly, to their children their own beliefs about gender. (p. 253)

An important Australian study by Antill, Cunningham, and Cotton (2003) indicated that the influence of parents on the gender roles adopted by their children was very significant and varied. First, demographic variables such as parents' education, religiosity, political allegiances, encouragement and tolerance of cross-gender interests and behaviours, and a non-traditional division of household chores were found to make a difference in the attitudes and gender role views of their children. Secondly, parents who reported a more traditional approach to child rearing (with the mother often staying at home and/or taking the responsibility for the majority of the basic care of the children), and who reported having attitudes towards gender which reflected this, in turn had children who tended towards these more traditional gender roles. Parents, then, impact the gender roles taken on by their children both in concrete deeds and attitudes, with the attitudes and roles adopted by children often reflecting those of their parents.

Earlier in this chapter the role of the media in promoting gender stereotypes for girls was discussed, but if scholars such at Witt (1997) are accurate, it is the home in which the seeds of such gender stereotypes are sown. If Witt's statement that the gender roles adopted are not always fair to children of both sexes is true, then the home is one important place in which this issue can be addressed. It is heartening to know from the results of studies such as the one by Antill et al. (2003) that children's gender roles and attitudes can be significantly shaped at home. Parents can and do influence their children in this regard, and the tolerance and encouragement of cross-gender behaviours, and fair redistribution of formerly gender-specific tasks, is one way parents can help to ensure that their children are equipped with the attitudes and secure gender identity to resist many of the gender stereotyped influences which they encounter outside of the home.

Window on Research

Booth and Amato (1994) conducted a longitudinal study including data collected over 12 years of 471 parents and their adult offspring to see if non-traditional gender roles and attitudes among parents are associated with later-life outcomes of children. A number of variables were used in the analysis, including psychological factors, the closeness of the relationship with parents of each gender, contact with parents, relationship and marriage questions, questions about friends, questions about self-esteem, and questions about non-traditional gender role attitudes. Other demographic variables such as age, race, education, and child gender were also factored into the analysis, which was conducted using the statistical procedure of multiple regression. Of particular note was the finding that 'family-of-origin nontraditionalism is significantly associated with offspring holding nontraditional gender role attitudes' (p. 872). Booth and Amato conclude with the statement that 'In contrast to the claims of those on the religious and political right, our research suggests that the current trend toward a less traditional, more egalitarian division of labor in the family poses relatively few problems for the youth of today' (p. 877).

Respecting children's differences at school

Schools in many parts of the world are struggling with how best to cater to children with diverse learning needs, however the historic antecedents that have led up to this point are still evident in most school systems. Schools and school systems have been traditionally structured around the (probably mythical) average student, representing the majority culture and religion, male gender, heterosexual orientation, and free of any form of ability-based exceptionality. This has resulted in school systems which, despite some changes, still tend to reflect that structure and those values. Those values and practices, however, are now facing a string of challenges.

Inclusive education for children with diverse learning needs

Polloway, Patton, Smith, and Smith (1996) identified four paradigms related to working with people with disabilities during the twentieth century. They argue that there was a shift from institutional ways of working with children who have disabilities (such as special schools and institutional living arrangements) towards more inclusive approaches later in the century, with segregated educational contexts being increasingly seen as less desirable. We are still, however, faced with a situation whereby the segregation of children with diverse abilities, including those with disabilities (but sometimes other issues such as language, cultural or religious differences) for educational purposes is seen by many as being in the best interests of everyone. Segregative school practices are still widely practiced in many areas of the world, including regions in some of the more developed nations such as parts of Canada, the United Kingdom, Australia, the United States, and Western and Eastern Europe. This is evident despite statements such as the following from the UK Ministry of Education (n.d.):

> Schools have a duty to promote equality of opportunity for all students and staff, regardless of their sexual orientation, race, religion or disability. This promotion of equality should be enshrined in school policies on equal opportunities, behaviour and the curriculum. (¶1)

The arguments made in favour of segregated schools and classrooms are generally that children in those settings will be taught by specially trained experts, and are usually in smaller classes. In this way, their needs will be better met than if they attend a regular classroom. Teachers in regular classes will have more time to teach students without exceptionalities, and there will be less disruption to learning in these classes. Furthermore, the argument is made that many parents want and demand such special classes, and this choice should be made available to them.

The above arguments, however, can be traced back to old ideas about who children from minority backgrounds, and specifically with disabilities, are. In a previous publication (Loreman, 2007a), I argued that Canadian educators tend to view children with disabilities in terms of deficits. If one focuses on what children are not able to do, and views them as primarily incompetent and in need of help, then separating them out into segregated classrooms for special help makes more sense. If one truly values children with disabilities, however, and recognizes their inherent strengths and capacities while acknowledging that all children are different in some way, then the justification for segregation becomes weaker. Where does one draw the line for who is and who is not segregated? Which children are worthy of education in a regular classroom, and which are not? Who has the moral right to make these decisions, and on what basis? There is no common agreement on the answers to these questions.

Supporters of inclusive education for children with disabilities have in the past been accused of acting on philosophical principles of social justice rather than justifying the approach in a pedagogical sense. This can no longer be said to be true. While research in the field continues, there is now strong support for the notion that inclusive education is a more effective approach for all children (including those without disabilities) in virtually every domain, including academic, social, and emotional, and that there are financial advantages for systems adopting this approach (Loreman, 2007b; Loreman, et al., 2005). Conversely, it might be asked where the research evidence is to support segregated educational contexts? The truth is that the research supporting this approach is now and always has been weak (Loreman, 2007b; Sobsey, 2005). Certainly, there are some studies which support the efficacy of some aspects of segregated education, however, given the long history of this approach (spanning over 100 years) one might expect more compelling evidence. This evidence simply does not exist.

Given the increasing popularity of inclusive education in recent years, many definitions of what the term means have been presented, and some of these definitions have been deliberately twisted so that the term inclusion has been used by some to mean whatever the practice happens to be in the region, some of which are most certainly not inclusive (Loreman, 1999). Take, for example, the teacher of a segregated classroom for children with autism who called her classroom inclusive because the children with autism were all there together. This is not inclusion. Uditsky (1993) provides a definition which is in agreement with the majority of supporters of inclusion:

> In the inclusive classroom the student with a significant disability, regardless of the degree or nature of that disability, is a welcomed and valued member. The student is: taught by the regular classroom teacher (who is supported as needed); follows the regular curriculum (with modification and adaptation); makes friends; and contributes to the learning of the entire class [and] . . . participates in all aspects of school life according to her interests and moves year to year with her peers from kindergarten through high school. (p. 79)

Using this definition as a basis, the faulty arguments supporting segregative school practices for children with differences can be exposed. The first argument, that children with differences will have their needs better met in a segregated setting, is not supported in the research literature. Indeed, the opposite is true. Children with disabilities have consistently demonstrated higher levels of academic achievement and greater engagement in inclusive settings, and this has been known for some time (Evans, Salisbury, Palombaro, & Goldberg,

1994; Frederickson, Dunsmuir, Lang, & Monsen, 2004; Hunt, Farron-Davis, Beckstead, Curtis, & Goetz, 1994; Sobsey, 2005). Further, children with disabilities who are included realize social advantages such as more friendships, and enhanced communication and social skill development (Bennett, DeLuca, & Bruns, 1997; Kennedy & Shukla, 1997). The assertion that the presence of children with disabilities has a negative impact on the learning of their non-disabled peers is similarly not supported by research. Not only has no measurable negative influence on academic progress for non-disabled peers been found (Davis, Langone, & Malone, 1996; Demeris, Childs, & Jordan, 2008; McDonnell, Thorson, McQuivey, & Kiefer-O'Donnell, 1997; Sharpe, York, & Knight, 1994), some studies have concluded that inclusion is advantageous for children without disabilities. For example, Cole, Waldron, and Majd (2004) found higher academic performance in math and Language Arts for children without disabilities if students with disabilities were present in the class. This is, of course, only a small sample of the available literature supporting the efficacy of inclusive education, but it is enough to demonstrate that inclusion clearly works and that the most common arguments against the approach do not hold up to scrutiny.

The third argument, that many parents want the choice of segregated education, also does not stand up to examination (especially given the arguments supporting the effectiveness of inclusive education above). For many parents segregated education is the only option, even in regions with a stated policy of inclusive education as the first and preferred option to be considered. In regular schools where parents of children with disabilities are not made to feel welcome, the choice for segregated settings becomes a forced choice. Many parents are simply not adequately informed about the advantages of inclusive education, or are told that the regular school must accept the child by law but that, really, the education provided by the special school down the road is much more appropriate to the needs of their child (Kenworthy & Whittaker, 2000). If inclusive education is being implemented well, and schools are positive about the participation of children with all types of difference in regular classes and are able to demonstrate success, very few parents will find a segregated setting desirable, thus eliminating the need for such choices.

In order to respect children with differences, regular schools need to work towards becoming inclusive, welcoming environments for all. The change is not easy, but inclusive education is a paradigm whose time has come. The ideas behind and practice of inclusive education have been around for well over 30 years now, and there is little excuse for present-day schools resisting this change. A plethora of resources exist to assist with the move towards inclusive education, and schools and school systems need to start taking greater advantages of those. Some systems, schools, and individual educators will protest that they are not yet ready for full inclusion. But if not now, then when?

Curriculum and support materials which include all

Another area of disregard for children's differences at school can be found in curriculum and the materials which support it. Although in recent times there has been an increased sensitivity to the need to include a plurality of viewpoints in school curricula and curriculum materials as they are revised, this has been a long time coming and is far from complete. American University Education Professor David Sadker (n.d.) suggests that seven forms of bias exist in instructional materials. These include:

- *Invisibility.* Certain groups are excluded from the discourse.
- *Stereotyping.* According to Sadker this 'assigns a rigid set of characteristics to all members of a group, at the cost of individual attributes and differences'.
- *Imbalance and selectivity.* This involves telling only part of the story; that part which highlights the majority view.
- *Unreality.* Ignoring unpleasant facts. In some ways this is similar to imbalance and selectivity, above, where only half the story is told. The need to recognize that social problems have existed and been overcome is important.
- *Fragmentation and isolation.* According to Sadker, this type of bias presents non-dominant groups as peripheral members of society. Often this amounts to limiting their inclusion in materials to special sections in those materials.
- *Linguistic bias.* Words that are used to exclude or discriminate against certain groups. For example, the word 'mankind' seemingly excludes women.
- *Cosmetic bias.* Instances where lip-service is given to the contributions of certain disadvantaged groups, without genuinely and fully exploring or outlining these contributions. (¶3)

While it is now less common to see blatant examples of racism and sexism in such materials than it was 20 years ago, some curriculum materials continue to reinforce the perspective of the dominant culture through the simple omission of other viewpoints. Ndura (2004) found that English as a Second Language (ESL) textbooks in the western United States were full of cultural biases along with missing, misconstrued, and misrepresented voices, and that further, the texts failed to empower students to identify these voices. Aside from presenting racial and cultural stereotypes (in one text a modern-day African boy who lives in a poor village is actually chased by a hungry lion!), these texts were also often gender biased in nature, and rendered some religious and ethnic groups invisible.

Even in instances where curriculum materials have been redeveloped to try and address issues of bias, this has not always been successful. A study by Yasemin (2007) found that revisions as part of the EU harmonization process to the Life Studies and Social Studies textbooks used in Turkish schools made little difference in terms of eliminating gender bias. According to Yasemin

> [The] new textbooks perform the function of reproducing gender segregation which was internalized by Turkish culture and the patriarchal ideology, by portraying men and women within their traditional roles. In this context, the extent to which this gender blind "curriculum reform" constitute a real reform in fact is questionable. (p. 15)

Despite some flawed attempts at curriculum and materials reform, there seems at least to be a recognition in the western educational community that this sort of bias is unacceptable. The issue that remains is the speed and competence with which these issues are dealt with.

Case Study: The Segregated Classroom

Brightlights school is a regular neighbourhood primary school that runs a segregated classroom for children with severe and multiple disabilities. The local school authority recently dropped the term 'segregated classroom' in favour of the term 'congregated classroom' to describe the programme as it felt this term was more palatable and current, although in general the way in which the classroom operates has not changed significantly in over 20 years. The classroom consists of 12 children aged 5–14 years with a wide variety of severe physical, cognitive, and developmental disabilities. Although not a designated programme for children with autism, one boy with autism is in the class as no other suitable placement could be found for him in the region. Most of the children live outside of the school's neighbourhood and are bussed in from other regions of the city each day. The class is staffed by a special education teacher, five teacher assistants, and a variety of therapists who visit the class on a consultative basis.

Most teaching and learning takes place within the context of the special classroom, and most of the programming is individual. The children tend to work individually or in small groups with the teacher or an assistant on specific objectives designed by the educational staff in consultation with the parents. The majority of the instruction is behavioural in nature involving positive and negative reinforcement schedules and task analysis (breaking large tasks to be taught into smaller steps). Occasionally, if deemed appropriate by all staff involved, some of the children join classes in the rest of the school for some subjects such as physical education, music, or art along with a staff member. This is known as integration time. They also get to see the other children in the school during the 15-minute morning recess and at school assemblies. Staff say this provides the children with the best of both worlds as they get the chance to interact with other children while also having their specific needs met in the segregated classroom.

Case Study—cont'd

The staff care deeply about these children and believe that in his context they can meet the majority of the physical needs of these students (including specialized feeding and toilet routines), along with providing them with an education in life skills such as dressing and cooking which they will need later in life. Both staff and parents say that the children in the class are happy to come to school each day, and are glad that they are somewhat protected from some of the teasing and bullying they say can occur in the regular classroom.

- In what ways does this segregated classroom differ from other classrooms?
- Examine the research literature. What does it say about the effectiveness of such classrooms?
- Does this way of educating show adequate respect for the children involved? How might some of the needs outlined above be addressed in an inclusive setting?

Respecting children's differences means both acknowledging that those differences exist, while at the same time not making them central to understandings about who the child is. Primarily, children are children, sharing a common humanity. All differences, however significant, are secondary considerations. This view may be seen as idealistic by some, but if a point is to be reached where acceptance is the norm, then this idea of humanity first and individual difference second must become a central feature and underlying foundation of all discourse on the topic.

Discussion Questions

- Examine the discrimination matrix (Table 6.3). Discuss real-life examples of discrimination described in each of the different boxes. Discuss the various types of participants and the methods you have seen used to achieve their goals.
- What sorts of things can be done to ameliorate the negative impact of gender role stereotyping in the home?
- Reflect on this text. What sorts of biases are evident? Are these biases made explicit?
- Consider and discuss the following questions relating to education posed earlier in this chapter: Where do we draw the line for who is and who is not segregated? Which children are worthy of education in a regular classroom and which are not? Who has the moral right to make these decisions and on what basis?

Further Resources

Fialka, J. (2005). *From puddles to pride: A mother's poems about her son, his disability, and her family's transformation*. (CD ROM). USA: danceofpartnership.com. For details go to www.danceofpartnership.com

David Sadker's website: www.american.edu/sadker/curricularbias.htm

Seskin, S., & Shamblin A. (2002). *Don't laugh at me*. Berkeley, CA: Tricycle Press.

Loreman, T., Deppeler, J., & Harvey, D. (2005). *Inclusive education: A practical guide to supporting diversity in the classroom*. Sydney: Allen & Unwin. (Published in the UK, USA and Canada by RoutledgeFalmer. Published in India by Viva Books.)

7 Conclusion
A model of respect for childhood

Having discussed some important features of childhood in the preceding chapters of this book, this concluding chapter will now try to briefly conceptualize a model of respect for childhood. There is no claim that the model to be outlined is in any way comprehensive, rather, the intent is that it should be viewed as a rough framework and a basis for discussion and modification as further ideas and research on the topic of respect for childhood become apparent.

Limits on respect for children

The preceding chapters have been written with the assumption that the basic needs of children have been previously met. This, however, is not always the case. Certain limitations, such as social conditions, can preclude the possibility of being able to implement many of the ideas discussed in this book. Maslow (1970), in his theory of human motivation, described a hierarchy of needs in which basic deficiency needs must be met before a person can be motivated to accomplish anything. These needs are physiological needs (such as shelter, clothing, food, and water), safety needs (both physical and psychological), love and belonging needs, and self-esteem needs. If these deficiency needs are not met, then any attempt to respect childhood along the lines suggested in this book will be significantly limited.

Restrictive social conditions

Poverty, as one example, is a social condition which precludes efforts to respect childhood. In fact, allowing children to exist in states of poverty in a world marked by regions of great affluence is shameful. UNICEF reports that 980 million children worldwide do not have access to adequate sanitation, and one in five babies in the developing world do not have access to a safe water supply (Ledwith, 2006). Statistics on child hunger and homelessness are equally grim. It is clear that children living in poverty have less time to engage in free play, are able to devote less time to relationships with their families, have reduced resources to support their capacities and abilities, and have significantly more stress in their lives than children who are not living in poverty. There are significant negative psychological, social, and developmental impacts associated with poverty (Flores, 2004; Molnar, Klein, Knitzer, & Oritz-Torres, 1988). How, for example, can a child who is hungry, tired, and stressed be expected to work productively with peers and maintain positive relationships? Children are certainly resilient and rich in resources, but as with all human beings there are limits to this resiliency. The same can be said for children living in war zones, children involved in child labour, children who are neglected, abused, and exploited, and children who are sick and unloved. Basic needs such as these have to be met before any progress can be made on promoting greater respect for children. Indeed, helping to see that these needs are met throughout the world is central to the work of respecting childhood on a global level.

Social conditions such as those described above, however, have been in existence for thousands of years, and despite our best efforts are unlikely to be fully eliminated any time soon. This is why context needs to be taken into account when trying to adjust to more respectful ways of working with children. More importantly, however, children living in such conditions can benefit from assistance provided by more affluent nations. One way of respecting childhood globally is for nations to provide financial and other forms of support for children in difficulty around the world, while at the same time using the democratic process to put pressure on governments and other agencies to find peaceful diplomatic, political, and social solutions to the problems at hand. International organizations such as the United Nations, UNESCO, the Red Cross, and countless others are attempting to help in this area with some success. Creating conditions in which childhood can be respected is one goal of the international community which is difficult not to support.

Resisting the pressures on childhood

Figure 7.1 outlines some of the pressures on respect for childhood discussed throughout this book. Currently, as has been discussed, some of the impact of each of these pressures is negative, and this negativity needs to be exposed

Figure 7.1 Pressures on respect for childhood

and actively resisted by both children and adults. Each of these pressures requires examination and reflection in order to retain the positive influences and eliminate the negative ones. Take, for example, technology. The judicious use of emerging technologies has many positive implications for improving childhood. However, there are many documented instances of technology being used inappropriately, to the detriment of children (see Chapter 3). As a further example in this area, a recent report from Japan shows that about a third of children aged 7–12 use cellular phones, with the number increasing to 96 per cent in High School. Many of these children communicate obsessively by text message (even where face-to-face interaction is an equally simple option), with some commenting that they are only connected to their friends via a machine (Suzuki, 2008). Most people would agree that authentic child-to-child relationships in this situation are under threat because of the misuse of such ubiquitous technology. Given this, something needs to be done. One is not powerless in the face of such pressures on respect for childhood unless one chooses to be through inaction and apathy. Adults have the power to help shape the lives of children, and this power should be exercised through the decisions made on their behalf. Using the above example, one could choose to keep ones children in the 4 per cent who do not have cellular phones, or perhaps more realistically let them use one, but restrict and monitor this use rigorously. This, of course, is just one example of how negative pressures on childhood can be resisted. The same line of thinking can be applied more broadly to the other pressure areas. Adults have power and so are obliged to use this power responsibly as advocates for children and childhood. In general, resisting negative pressure on childhood is not easy, but principled stands and action are essential if meaningful positive changes to how children are viewed, treated, and respected are to be made.

A model of respect for childhood

Having read this book, one might be forgiven for asking for a Borba-esque list of ways of working and living with children in ways which are respectful to them. None has been provided, and the truth is, none exists. As is evident in the discussion throughout this text, children are complex and unique, and something as simple as a prescription for working with them would always be inadequate. Instead, this book offers broad considerations for working with children based on three general principles. These principles are:

1. protect children
2. support children
3. leave children alone.

Three principles for living and working with children

Figure 7.2 illustrates the three principles of working and living with children which have formed the underlying philosophy of this book. First and foremost is the need to protect children. This acts as the foundation upon which supporting children and leaving them alone can be carefully balanced and negotiated.

While at times this book has advocated backing away from high levels of interference in the lives of children, this does not imply that adults are not central to their lives. Indeed, it is essential that adults provide children with the protection they need against many of the problems of society outlined in Figure 7.2 such as exploitation and abuse. It is our moral and legal

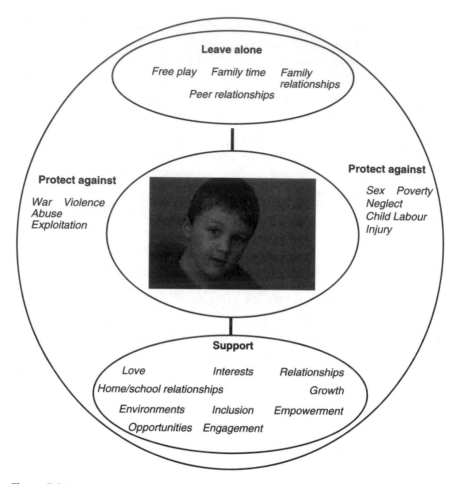

Figure 7.2 Essential elements for supporting respect for children

responsibility to do so, and in fulfilling this role adults help to preserve what is important about childhood. Without a solid basis of physical and psychological safety nothing else can be accomplished.

The bluntly phrased principle of leaving children alone has received significant attention throughout this book. Over the years, adults in western society have increasingly interfered in the lives of children, sometimes well over and above what is necessary for providing physical and psychological safety or sensible levels of support. One of the central themes of this book is that adults need to recognize when it is important to back away, and allow children to experience childhood on their own terms. Adults need to allow children the space (temporal, physical, and psychological) to explore and interact with the world in ways dictated by them. Adults need to reconsider the value of free play, free time, and free association. These provide children with rich, meaningful, personal opportunities for enjoyment and growth.

Finally, it is not enough to simply provide protection and leave children alone. Under these circumstances children would be cut adrift, unable to adequately make sense of and function in a complex world. Adults need to offer and provide children with support as they grow and learn. At its heart, this support involves providing love. If we love the children in our lives, and they know that they are loved and that this will never be withdrawn, then they have a basis for exploration, finding success, and making mistakes. They will take risks they might not otherwise take, knowing that they have a safety net in the form of the adults in their lives. We need to provide them with opportunity, with authentic environments, and scaffolds on which they can build their own understandings of the world. This is always going to be a difficult balancing act. Support needs to be provided without having it lapse into too much interference. Helping a child to learn to ride a bicycle is a good metaphor for this. We run along beside them and gradually reduce our hold on the bike until the child is able to ride by herself. She may fall, but we will be there to help her get up and try again. If we never let go of the bike, or if we pedal and steer it for her, she will never learn how to ride.

References

Albert, L. (2003). *Cooperative discipline* (Rev. edn). Minnesota: AGS.

American School & University. (2007). Playground injuries. *American School & University, 80*(2), 10.

Anderson, C. A., Berkowitz, L., Donnerstein, E., Huesman, L. R., Johnson, J. D., Linz, D., et al. (2003). The influence of media violence on youth. *Psychological Science in the Public Interest, 4,* 81–110.

Antill, J. K., Cunningham, J. D., & Cotton, S. (2003). Gender-role attitudes in middle childhood: In what ways do parents influence their children? *Australian Journal of Psychology, 55*(3), 148–53.

Aurelius, M. (2006). *The meditations of Marcus Aurelius.* London: Watkins.

Austin, E. (1998). Who needs recess? *Child, 13*(7), 88.

Bailey, L. B. (2006). Interactive homework: A tool for fostering parent–child interactions and improving learning outcomes for at-risk young children. *Early Childhood Education Journal, 34*(2), 155–67.

Baird, J. R. (1984). *Improved learning through enhanced metagognition.* Unpublished doctoral dissertation, Monash University, Melbourne.

Baird, J. R., & Northfield, J. R. (1995). *Learning from the PEEL experience.* Melbourne, Australia: Monash University.

Baker, A. J. L., Kessler-Sklar, S., Piotrkowski, C. S., & Lamb Parker, F. (1999). Kindergarten and first-grade teachers' reported knowledge of parents' involvement in their children's education. *The Elementary School Journal, 99*(4), 367–80.

Baker, B. L., Brightman, A. J., & Blacher, J. B. (2004). *Steps to independence: Teaching everyday skills to children with special needs* (4th edn). Baltimore: Brookes.

Bandura, A. (1973). *Aggression: A social learning analysis.* Englewood Cliffs, NJ: Prentice Hall.

Bandura, A. (1977). *Social learning theory.* Englewood Cliffs, NJ: Prentice Hall.

Bandura, A. (1986). *Social foundations of thought and action: A social cognitive theory.* Englewood Cliffs, NJ: Prentice Hall.

Bandura, A., & Walters. R. H. (1959). *Adolescent aggression: A study of the influence of child-training practices and family interrelationships.* New York: Ronald Press.

Barlow, J., Abbs, P., Albrecht, K. M., Alladin, W., Allison, C., Almon, J., et al. (2007, September 10). Let our children play. *Daily Telegraph.* Retrieved 3 November 2007, from http://www.telegraph.co.uk/opinion/main.jhtml;jsessionid=FAQ35TZLO4I3RQFIQMFCFFWAVCBQYIV0?xml=/opinion/2007/09/10/nosplit/dt1001.xml

Bennett, T., DeLuca, D., & Bruns, D. (1997). Putting inclusion into practice: Perspectives of teachers and parents. *Exceptional Children, 64*(11), 115–31.

Bernanke, B. S. (2007, September). *Education and economic competitiveness.* Speech made at the US Chamber Education and Workforce Summit, Washington, DC. Retrieved 16 October 2007, from http://www.federalreserve.gov/newsevents/speech/bernanke20070924a.htm

Blok, H. (2004). Performance in home schooling: An argument against compulsory schooling in the Netherlands. *International Review of Education, 50*(1), 39–52.

Bonetti, R., & Filippini, T. (2001). The right hand. In C. Giudici, C. Rinaldi, & M. Krechevsky (eds), *Making learning visible: Children as individual and group learners* (pp. 34–37). Reggio Emilia, Italy: Reggio Children and Project Zero.

Booth, A., & Amato, P. R. (1994). Parental gender role nontraditionalism and offspring outcomes. *Journal of Marriage and the Family, 56*(4), 865–77.

Borba, M. (2004). *Don't give me that attitude!: 24 rude, selfish, insensitive things kids do and how to stop them.* San Francisco: John Wiley.

Bornstein, M. H. (2005). Parenting matters. *Infant and Child Development, 14*, 311–14.

Bradley, P. (1995). Media leaders and personal ideology. *Journalism History, 21*(2), 79–87.

Broadbent, A. (2006, March). *The world we want: Celebrating community and living together.* Paper presented at Philia Community Dialogue on Citizenship, Edmonton, Alberta.

Bronfenbrenner, U. (1979). *The ecology of human development: Experiments by nature and design.* Cambridge, MA: Harvard University Press.

Bruner, J. (1966). *Toward a theory of instruction.* Cambridge, MA: Harvard University Press.

Bruner, J. (1986). *Actual minds, possible worlds.* Boston: Harvard University Press.

Bruner, J. (1998). Some specifications for a space to house a Reggio preschool. In G. Ceppi & M. Zini. (eds), *Children, spaces, relations: Metaproject for an environment for young children* (p. 138). Reggio Emilia, Italy: Reggio Children and Domus Academy Research Centre.

Byrd, R. S., Weitzman, M., & Auinger, P. (1997). Increased behavior problems associated with delayed school entry and delayed school progress. *Pediatrics, 100*(4), 654–61.

Campbell, C. P. (1995). *Race, myth and the news.* London: Sage.

Canadian Council on Learning. (2007). *2007 Survey of Canadian attitudes toward learning: Results for elementary and secondary school learning.* Ottawa, Ontario: Canadian Council on Learning. Retrieved 7 December 2007, from www.ccl-cca.ca/scal

Carbone, A., Hurst, J., Mitchell, I., & Gunstone, R. (1999). The student learning experience: Characteristics of programming tasks that lead to the poor learning behaviours. *Proceedings of the HERDSA Annual International Conference on Learning.*

Carnagey, N. L., & Anderson, C. A. (2005). The effects of reward and punishment in violent video games on aggressive affect, cognition, and behaviour. *Psychological Science, 16*(11), 882–89.

Carr, D. (2007). Towards and educationally meaningful curriculum: Epistemic holism and knowledge integration revisited. *British Journal of Educational Studies, 55*(1), 3–20.

Castagnetti, M., & Vecchi, V. (eds). (1997). *The unheard voice of children: Shoe and meter* (L. Morrow, Trans.). Reggio Emilia, Italy: Reggio Children.

Ceppi, G., & Zini, M. (eds). (1998). *Children, spaces, relations: Metaproject for an environment for young children.* Reggio Emilia, Italy: Reggio Children and Domus Academy Research Centre.

Cheung, S. K., & Leung Ngai, J. M. Y. (1992). Impact of homework stress on children's physical and psychological well-being. *Journal of the Hong Kong Medical Association, 44*(3), 146–50.

Colby, A., Gibbs, J., Lieberman, M., & Kohlberg, L. (1983). *A longitudinal study of moral judgment: A monograph for the society of research in child development.* Chicago: The University of Chicago Press.

Cole, C. M., Waldron, N., & Majd, M. (2004). Academic programs of students across inclusive and traditional settings. *Mental Retardation, 42*(2), 136–44.

Collins, T. (2005). *First Nations, Metis, and Inuit education.* Presented at Concordia University College of Alberta, November 2005.

Cosden, M., Morrison, G., Gutierrez, L., & Brown, M. (2004). The effects of homework programs and after-school activities on student success. *Theory into Practice, 43*(3), 220–26.

Dahlberg, G., Moss, P., & Pence, A. (1999). *Beyond quality in early childhood education and care: Postmodern perspectives.* Philadelphia: Falmer Press.

Daniels, E. A., & Leaper, C. (2006). *Media representations of active women: What are girls seeing and does it affect their self-concept?* Unpublished doctoral dissertation, University of California – Santa Cruz.

Darling, N. (2005). Participation in extracurricular activities and adolescent adjustment: Cross-sectional and longitudinal findings. *Journal of Youth and Adolescence, 34*(5), 493–505.

Davis, M. T., Langone, J., & Malone, D. M. (1996). Promoting prosocial behaviours among preschool children with and without disabilities. *International Journal of Disability, Development and Education, 43*(3), 219–46.

DeGaetano, G. (2005). The impact of media violence on developing minds and hearts. In S. Olfman (ed.), *Childhood lost: How American culture is failing our kids* (pp. 89–106). Westport, CT: Praeger/Greenwood.

Demeris, H., Childs, R. A., & Jordan, A. (2008). The influence of students with special needs included in Grade 3 classrooms on the large-scale achievement scores of students with special needs. *Canadian Journal of Education, 30*(3), 609–27.

Dennison, G. (1969). *The lives of children: The story of the first Street School.* New York: Random House.

Derevensky, J. (2008, April 19). [Review of the book *Under pressure: Rescuing childhood from the culture of hyper-parenting*]. *National Post* (Canada), WP17.

DeVries, R. (2000). Vygotsky, Piaget and education: A reciprocal assimilation of theories and educational practices. *New Ideas in Psychology, 18*(3), 187–213.

Dewey, J. (1894). My pedagogic creed. *The School Journal, 54*(3), 77–80.

Doll, W. (1993). *A postmodern perspective on curriculum.* New York: Teachers College Press.

Dubanoski, R., Inaba, M., & Gerkewics, K. (1983). Corporal punishment in schools: Myths, problems and alternatives. *Child Abuse and Neglect, 7,* 271–78.

Dubroc, A. (2007). *Is the elimination of recess in school a violation of a child's basic human rights?* USA: American Intercontinental University. (ERIC Document Reproduction Service No. ED495814).

Elkind, D. (1981). *The hurried child.* Cambridge, MA: Da Capo.

Elkind, D. (2007). *The hurried child: Growing up too fast too soon* (25th anniversary edn). Cambridge, MA: Da Capo.

eMarketer. (2007). *Demographics and usage/internet users/children.* Accessed November 7, 2007, from www.emarketer.com

Emmett, J., & Harry, R. (2003). *Ruby in her own time.* New York: Scholastic.

Erikson, E. (1968). *Identity, youth, and crisis.* New York: Norton.

Erikson, E. (1980). *Identity and the life cycle.* New York: Norton.

Esdaile, S. A., & Greenwood, K. M. (2003). A comparison of mother's and father's experience of parenting stress and attributions for parent–child interaction outcomes. *Occupational Therapy International, 10*(2), 115–26.

Evans, I. M., Salisbury, C., Palombaro, M., & Goldberg, J. S. (1994). Children's perception of fairness in classroom and interpersonal situations involving peers with severe disabilities. *Journal of the Association for Persons with Severe Handicaps, 19*(4), 326–32.

Farbman, D. (2007). A new day for kids. *Educational Leadership, 64*(8), 62–65.

Favre, C., & Bizzini, L. (1995). Some contributions of Piaget's genetic epistemology and psychology to cognitive therapy. *Clinical Psychology & Psychotherapy, 2*(1), 15–23.

Feder, J., Levant, R. F., & Dean, J. (2007). Boys and violence: A gender-informed analysis. *Professional Psychology: Research and Practice, 38*(4), 385–91.

Fialka, J. (2005). *From puddles to pride: A mother's poems about her son, his disability, and her family's transformation.* (CD ROM). USA: danceofpartnership.com

Fineman, M. (2004). *The autonomy myth: A theory of dependency.* New York: New York Press.

Flores, R. (2004). The effect of poverty on young children's ability to organize everyday events. *Journal of Children & Poverty, 10*(2), 99–118.

Forman, G., & Fyfe, B. (1998). Negotiated learning through design, documentation, and discourse. In C. Edwards, L. Gandini, & G. Forman (eds), *The hundred languages of children: The Reggio Emilia approach – advanced reflections* (pp. 239–60). Connecticut: Ablex.

Frederickson, N., Dunsmuir, S., Lang, J., & Monsen, J. J. (2004). Mainstream-special school inclusion partnerships: Pupil, parent and teacher perspectives. *International Journal of Inclusive Education, 8*(1), 37–57.

Fulligni, A., & Hardaway, C. (2007). Preparing diverse adolescents for the transition to adulthood. *The Future of Children, 14*(2), 99–119.

Furnham, A., Abramsky, S., & Gunter, B. (1997). A cross-cultural content analysis of children's television advertisements. *Sex Roles, 37*(1/2), 91–99.

Gandini, L. (1998). Educational and caring spaces. In C. Edwards, L. Gandini, & G. Forman (eds), *The hundred languages of children: The Reggio Emilia approach – advanced reflections* (pp. 161–78). Connecticut: Ablex.

Gardner, H. (1983). *Frames of mind: The theory of multiple intelligences*. New York: Basic Books.

Gardner, H. (1999). *Intelligence reframed*. New York: Basic Books.

Gardner, H., & Boix-Mansilla, V. (1994). Teaching for understanding in the disciplines – and beyond. *Teachers College Record, 96*(2), 198–218.

Gardner, H., & Moran, S. (2006). The science of multiple intelligences theory: A response to Lynne Waterhouse. *Educational Psychologist, 41*(4), 227–32.

Gilbert, S. (1999, August 3). For some children, it's an after-school pressure cooker. *New York Times, 148*(51603), F7.

Gilman, R., Meyers, J., & Perez, L. (2004). Structured extracurricular activities among adolescents : Findings and implications for school psychologists. *Psychology in the Schools, 41*(1), 31–41.

Ginsburg, K. R., The Committee on Communications, & The Committee on Psychosocial Aspects of Child and Family Health. (2006). Clinical report: The importance of play in promoting healthy child development and maintaining strong parent–child bonds. *Pediatrics, 119*(1), 182–91.

Gleeson, T. R., & Hohmann, L. M. (2006). Concepts of real and imaginary friendships in early childhood. *Social Development, 15*(1), 128–44.

Global Initiative to End All Corporal Punishment of Children. (2007). *Global summary of legal status of corporal punishment of children*. Retrieved 13 December 2007, from http://www.endcorporalpunishment.org/pages/pdfs/charts/Chart-Global.pdf

Gonzalez, A.-L., & Wolters, C. A. (2006). The relation between perceived parenting practices and achievement motivation in mathematics. *Journal of Research in Childhood Education, 21*(2), 203–17.

Graue, M. E., & DiPerna, J. (2004). Redshirting and early retention: Who gets the 'gift of time' and what are its outcomes? *American Educational Research Journal, 37*(2), 509–34.

Green, C. L., & Hoover-Dempsey, K. V. (2007). Why do parents homeschool? *Education & Urban Society, 39*(2), 264–85.

Greenspan, B. (1978). *Children through the ages: A history of childhood*. New York: Barnes & Noble.

Griggs, S., & Griggs, C. (1993). Alternative hours: A response to increased pressure upon pupils and staff at Willingdon School, East Sussex. *School Organisation, 13*(2), 199–212.

Groth, M. (2007). 'Has anyone seen the boy?': The fate of the boy in becoming a man. *Thymos: Journal of Boyhood Studies, 1*(1), 6–42.

Haidt, J. (2001). The emotional dog and it's rational tail: A social intuitionist approach to moral judgment. *Psychological Review, 108*, 814–34.

Haller, B., Dorries, B., & Rahn, J. (2006). Media labeling versus the US disability community identity: A study of shifting cultural language. *Disability & Society, 21*(1), 61–75.

Hambrook, J., Jordan, A., Rice, R., Koch, B. M., Richardson, B., & Huang, C. (2007). Give school's more time. *American School Board Journal, 194*(11), 15–16.

Hartley-Brewer, E. (2006). Afterschool adventures. *Scholastic Parent & Child*, October, 2006, 66–67.

Hastings, R. P., & Johnson, E. (2001). Stress in UK families conducting intensive home-based behavioral intervention for their young child with autism. *Journal of Autism & Developmental Disorders, 31*(3), 327–36.

Heitzmann, R. (2007). Target homework to maximize learning. *Education Digest.* March issue.

Holt, J. (1972). *Freedom and beyond.* New York: Dutton.

Holt, J. (1989). *Learning all the time.* New York: Addison Wesley.

Honore, C. (2008). *Under pressure: Rescuing childhood from the culture of hyper-parenting.* Toronto: Knopf Canada.

Howard, A. W., MacArthur, C., Willan, A., Rothman, L., Moses-McKeag, A., & MacPherson, A. K. (2005). The effect of safer play equipment on playground injury rates among school children. *Canadian Medical Association Journal, 172*(11), 1443–46.

Hunt, P., Farron-Davis, F., Beckstead, S., Curtis, D., & Goetz, L. (1994). Evaluating the effects of placement on students with severe disabilities in general education versus special classes. *The Journal of the Association for Persons with Severe Handicaps, 19*(3), 200–14.

Hunter, S., & Sundel, M. (1989). Introduction: An examination of key issues concerning midlife. In S. Hunter & M. Sundel. (eds), *Midlife myths: Issues, findings, and practice implications* (pp. 4–13). Newbury Park: Sage.

Johnson, A. (2007). The subtleties of blatant sexism. *Communication & Critical/Cultural Studies, 4*(2), 166–83.

Johnson, E., & Hastings, R. P. (2002). Facilitating factors and barriers to the implementation of intensive home-based behavioural intervention for young children with autism. *Child: Care, Health and Development, 28*(2), 123–29.

Jones, P., & Gloeckner, G. (2004). First year college performance: A study of home school graduates and traditional school graduates. *Journal of College Admission, 183,* 17–20.

Jordan, A. B., Hersey, J. C., McDivitt, J. A., & Heitzler, C. D. (2006). Reducing children's television-viewing time: A qualitative study of parents and their children, *Pediatrics, 118*(5), e1303–e1310.

Kama, A. (2004). Supercrips versus the pitiful handicapped: Reception of disabling images by disabled audience members. *Communications: The European Journal of Communication Research, 29*(4), 447–66.

Kang, S. (2007). Disembodiment in online social interaction: Impact of online chat on social support and psychosocial well-being. *CyberPsychology & Behavior, 10*(3), 475–77.

Kao, Chin-Cheng. (2001). Children's stress and after-school lives in Taiwan. *Dissertation Abstracts International, 62*(4-B), 2093.

Kavkler, M., Aubrey, C., & Tancig, S. (2000). Getting it right from the start? The influence of early school entry on later achievements in mathematics. *European Early Childhood Education Research Journal, 8*(1), 75–93.

Kennedy, C. H., & Shukla, S. (1997). Comparing the effects of educational placement on the social relationships of intermediate school students with severe disabilities. *Exceptional Children, 64*(1), 31–48.

Kenworthy, J., & Whittaker, J. (2000). Anything to declare? The struggle for inclusive education and children's rights. *Disability & Society, 15*(2), 219–31.

King, J., & Hicks, L. (2007). What ever happened to 'What might have been?' *American Psychologist, 62*(7), 625–36.

Klausen, E., & Passman, R. H. (2007). Pretend companions (imaginary playmates): The emergence of a field. *Journal of Genetic Psychology, 167*(4), 349–64.

Kohlberg, L. (1971). *From is to ought: How to commit the naturalistic fallacy and get away with it in the study of moral development.* New York: Academic Press.

Kohlberg, L. (1976). Moral stages and moralization: The cognitive-developmental approach. In L. Kohlberg & T. Lickona (eds), *Moral Development and Behavior: Theory, Research and Social Issues* (pp. 31–48). New York: Rinehart and Winston.

Kohlberg, L. (1984). *Essays in moral development: Vol 2. The psychology of moral development.* New York: Harper & Row.

Kohn, A. (2006a). Abusing research: The study of homework and other examples. *Phi Delta Kappan, (88)*1. Retrieved 16 October 2007, from www.alfiekohn.com

Kohn, A. (2006b). Down with homework. *Instructor, 116*(2). Retrieved 31 October 2007, from www.alfiekohn.com

Kohn, A. (2006c). *The homework myth: Why our kids get too much of a bad thing.* Cambridge, MA: Da Capo Books.

Kohn, A. (2007a). Rethinking homework. *Principal.* Retrieved 31 October 2007, from www.alfiekohn.com

Kohn, A. (2007b). Changing the homework default. *Independent School, 66*(2). Retrieved 16 October 2007, from www.alfiekohn.com

Koyama, R., Takahashi, Y., & Mori, K. (2006). Assessing the cuteness of children: Significant factors and gender differences. *Social Behaviour and Personality, 34*(9), 1087–1100.

Kravtsova, M. M. (2006). A comparative analysis of the moral judgments of younger students. *Russian Education & Society, 48*(12), 64–81.

Krcmar, M., & Hight, A. (2007). The development of aggressive mental models in young children. *Media Psychology, 10*(2), 250–69.

Krebs, D. L., & Denton, K. (2005). Toward a more pragmatic approach to morality: A critical evaluation of Kohlberg's model. *Psychological Review, 112*(3), 629–49.

Krebs, D. L., & Denton, K. (2006). Explanatory limitations of cognitive-developmental approaches to morality. *Psychological Review, 113*(3), 672–75.

Krebs, D. L., Denton, K., & Wark, G. (1997). The forms and functions of real-life moral decision-making. *Journal of Moral Education, 26*(2), 131–45.

Kuntsche, E. N. (2004). Hostility among adolescents in Switzerland? Multivariate relations between excessive media use and forms of violence. *Journal of Adolescent Health, 34*, 230–36.

Kyriakides, L. (2005). Evaluating school policy on parents working with their children in class. *Journal of Educational Research, 98*(5), 281–98.

Lawson, A. E., & Wollman, W. T. (2003). Encouraging the transition from concrete to formal cognitive functioning: An experiment. *Journal of Research in Science Teaching, 40*(Special issue), S33–S50.

Lebeda, S. (2007). Homeschooling: Depriving children of social development? *The Journal of Contemporary legal Issues, 16*(1), 99–104.

LeBesco, K. (2006). Disability, gender and difference on The Sopranos. *Women's Studies in Communication, 29*(1), 39–58.

Ledwith, T. (2006). *Progress for children reports mixed results on access to water and sanitation worldwide.* Los Angeles: UNICEF. Retrieved 16 January 2008, from http://www.unicefusa.org/site/c.duLRI8O0H/b.1700383/k.6AC6/Progress_for_Children.htm

Lee, M. (2007). Spark up the American Revolution with math, science, and more: An example of an integrative curriculum unit. *Social Studies, 98*(4), 159–64.

Leeds, A. (2005). Independence as a goal of education: Why we need less of it. *Encounter: Education for Meaning and Social Justice, 18*(3), 50–56.

Leonie, V. (2005, February 21). Horrible homework. *The Melbourne Age Online.* Retrieved 31 October 2007, from http://www.education.theage.com.au/pagedetail.asp?intpageid=1429&strsection=students&intsectionid=0

Leung, L. (2007). Stressful life events, motives for internet use, and social support among digital kids. *CyberPsychology & Behavior, 10*(2), 204–14.

Link, B., & Phelan, J. (2001). Conceptualising stigma. *Annual Review of Sociology, 27,* 363–85.

Loreman, T. (1999). Integration: Coming from the outside. *Interaction, 13*(1), 21–23.

Loreman, T. (2007a). How we view young children with diverse abilities: What Canada can learn from Reggio Emilia. *Exceptionality Education Canada, 17*(1), 5–26.

Loreman, T. (2007b). Seven pillars of support for inclusive education: Moving from 'Why?' to 'How?' *International Journal of Whole Schooling, 3*(2), 22–38.

Loreman, T., Deppeler, J., & Harvey, D. (2005). *Inclusive education: A practical guide to supporting diversity in the classroom.* Sydney: Allen & Unwin.

Lorenco, O., & Muchado, A. (1996). In defense of Piaget's theory: A reply to 10 common criticisms. *Psychological Review, 103*(1), 143–64.

Lubienski, C. (2003). A critical view of home education. *Evaluation & Research in Education, 17*(2/3), 167–78.

Luthar, S. S., Shoum, K. A., & Brown, P. J. (2006). Extracurricular involvement among affluent youth: A scapegoat for 'ubiquitous achievement pressures'? *Developmental Psychology, 42*(3), 583–97.

Mahoney, J. L. (2000). School extracurricular activity participation as a moderator in the development of antisocial patterns. *Child Development, 71*(2), 502–16.

Mahoney, J. L., Harris, A. L., Eccles, J. S., Elkind, D., Cloud, J., & The American Association of Pediatrics. (2007). The overscheduled child? *Chronicle of Higher Education, 53*(28), B4.

Maier, T. (1998). *Dr. Spock: An American life.* New York: Harcourt Brace.

Malaguzzi, L. (1998). History, ideas and basic philosophy: An interview with Lella Gandini. In C. Edwards, L. Gandini, & G. Forman (eds), *The hundred languages of children: The Reggio Emilia approach – advanced reflections* (pp. 49–98). Connecticut: Ablex.

Malone, K. (2007). The bubble-wrap generation: Children growing up in walled gardens. *Environmental Education Research, 13*(4), 513–27.

Malone, K., & Tranter, P. (2005). 'Hanging out in the schoolground': A reflective look at researching children's environmental learning, *Canadian Journal of Environmental Education, 10,* 212–24.

Mamen, M. (2006). *The pampered child syndrome: How to recognize it, how to manage it, and how to avoid it'* (Rev. edn). London: Jessica Kingsley Publishers.

Martin, M. O., Gonzalez, E. J., & Chrostowski, S. J. (2004). *Findings from IEA's trends in international mathematics and science study at the Fourth and Eighth Grades.* Chestnut Hill, MA: TIMSS & PIRLS International Study Center, Boston College.

Maslow, A. H. (1970). *Motivation and personality* (Rev. edn). New York: Harper & Row.

Mason, M. (2005). A society that cuts its parents adrift. *Community Care, 1590,* 22.

May, D. C., & Kundert, D. K. (1995). Does delayed school entry reduce later grade retentions and use of special education services? *Remedial & Special Education, 16*(5), 288–94.

McDonnell, J., Thorson, N., McQuivey, C., & Kiefer-O'Donnell, R. (1997). Academic engaged time of students with low-incidence disabilities in general education classes. *Mental Retardation, 35*(1), 18–26.

McKendrick, J. H., Bradford, M. G., & Fielder A. V. (2000). Kid customer? Commercialization of playspace and the commoditization of childhood. *Childhood, 7*(3), 295–314.

McNally, J., I'anson, J., Whewell, C., & Wilson, G. (2005). 'They think that swearing is okay': First lessons in behaviour management. *Journal of Education for Teaching, 31*(3), 169–85.

McTighe, J., Seif, E., & Wiggins, G. (2004). You can teach for meaning. *Educational Leadership, 62*(1), 26–30.

Medlin, R. (2000). Home schooling and the question of socialization. *Peabody Journal of Education, 75*(1/2), 107–23.

Meister, D. G., & Nolan, J. (2001). Out on a limb on our own: Uncertainty and doubt in moving from subject-centered to interdisciplinary teaching. *Teachers College Record, 103*(4), 608–33.

Mercogliano, C. (1998). *Making it up as we go along: The story of the Albany Free School.* Portsmouth, NH: Heinemann.

Miles, C. (2004). Going back to school. *Paths of Learning, 19,* 29–33.

Milevsky, A., Schlechter, M., Netter, S., & Keehn, D. (2007). Maternal and paternal parenting styles in adolescents: Associations with self-esteem, depression and life-satisfaction. *Journal of Child & Family Studies, 16*(1), 39–47.

Merriam Webster Online Dictionary. (n.d.). *Merriam Webster Online Dictionary.* Retrieved 17 October 2007, from http://www.m-w.com/dictionary

Molland, J. (2004). High-speed kids. *Parents, 79*(5), 213–14.

Molnar, J., Klein, T., Knitzer, J., & Oritz-Torres, B. (1988). *Home is where the heart is: The crisis of homeless children and their families in New York City.* New York: Bank Street College of Education.

Moran, P., & Ghate, D. (2005). The effectiveness of parenting support. *Children & Society, 19*(4), 329–36.

Morrison, K. A. (2007). Unschooling: Homeschools can provide the freedom to learn. *Encounter: Education for Meaning and Social Justice, 20*(2), 42–49.

Morrongiello, B. A., Corbett, M., Lasenby, J., Johnston, N., & McCourt, M. (2006). Factors influencing young children's risk of unintentional injury: Parenting style and strategies for teaching about home safety. *Journal of Applied Developmental Psychology, 27*(6), 560–70.

Morton, L. L., & Courneya, N. M. (1990). Early school entry and subsequent academic problems. *Alberta Journal of Educational Research, 36*(4), 311–23.

n.a. (2004a). France's hijab ban. *CBC News Online*. Retrieved 25 May 2008, from http://www.cbc.ca/news/background/islam/hijab.html

n.a. (2004b). First girls expelled over French headscarf ban. *CBC News Online*. Retrieved 25 May 2008, from http://www.cbc.ca/story/world/national/2004/10/20/france_headscarves041020.html

National Assembly and Senate of France. (2004). *LOI No. 2004-228 du 15 mars 2004 encadrant, en application du principe de laïcité, le port de signes ou de tenues manifestant une appartenance religieuse dans les écoles, collèges et lycées publics*. Retrieved 25 May 2008, from http://www.legifrance.gouv.fr

Ndura, E. (2004). ESL and cultural bias: An analysis of elementary through high school textbooks in the western United States of America. *Language, Culture and Curriculum, 17*(2), 143–53.

Newcombe, N., & Huttenlocher, J. (1992). Children's ability to solve perspective-taking problems. *Developmental Psychology, 28*, 635–43.

Nimmo, J. (1998). The child in community: Constraints from the early childhood lore. In C. Edwards, L. Gandini, & G. Forman. (eds), *The hundred languages of children: The Reggio Emilia approach – advanced reflections* (pp. 295–312). Connecticut: Ablex.

Nobes, G., & Smith, M. (1997). Physical punishment of children in two-parent families. *Clinical Child Psychology and Psychiatry, 2*(2), 271–81.

Ogata, A. (2005). Creative playthings. *Winterthur Portfolio, 39*(2/3), 130–56.

Ormrod, J. E., Saklofske, D. H., Schwean, V. L., Harrison, G. L., & Andrews, J. W. (2006). *Principles of educational psychology*. Toronto: Prentice Hall.

Orwell, G. (1935). *The clergyman's daughter*. London: Penguin Books.

Patterson, G. R., DeBaryshe, B. D., & Ramsey, E. (1989). A developmental perspective on antisocial behavior. *American Psychologist, 44*(2), 329–35.

Pearson, D., Rouse, H., Doswell, S., Ainsworth, D., Dawson, O., Simms, K., et al. (2001). Prevalence of imaginary companions in a normal child population. *Child: Care, Health and Development, 27*(1), 13–22.

Peterson, M., & Loreman, T. (2005, April). *Walking and talking the road to trusting community: Relationship-based schoolwide positive behavioural supports*. Presented at the Whole Schooling Conference 2005, Edmonton, Alberta.

Peterson, M., & Tamor, L. (2003). *Creating schools that work: Creating excellence and equity for a democratic society*. Detroit: Whole Schooling Press.

Pettit, G. S., Harrist, A. W., Bates, J. E., & Dodge, K. A. (1991). Family interaction, social cognition, and children's subsequent relations with peers at kindergarten. *Journal of Social and Personal Relationships, 8*, 383–402.

Piaget, J. (1929). *The child's conception of the world.* New York: Harcourt Brace.

Piaget, J. (1952). *The origins of intelligence in children.* New York: Norton.

Piaget, J. (1959). *Judgment and reasoning in the child.* New Jersey: Littlefield Adams.

Piaget, J. (1970). *Structuralism.* New York: Harper & Row.

Platt, S. (Ed.). (1989). *Respectfully quoted: A dictionary of quotations requested from the Congressional Research Service.* Washington, DC: Library of Congress.

Polloway, E. A., Patton, J. R., Smith, J. D., & Smith, T. E. C. (1996). Historic changes in mental retardation and developmental disabilities. *Education & Training in Mental Retardation, 31*(1), 3–12.

Pridmore, J. (2007). George MacDonald's estimate of childhood. *International Journal of Children's Spirituality, 12*(1), 61–74.

Prinsen, J., & Hellendorn, J. (1989). Imaginary companions: Do they still exist? *Kind en Adolescent, 10*(1), 42–48.

Qualifications and Curriculum Authority. (n.d.). *United Kingdom national curriculum.* UK: Qualifications and Curriculum Authority. Retrieved 31 October 2007, from http://curriculum.qca.org.uk/aims/index.aspx

Ravet, J. (2007). Making sense of disengagement in the primary classroom: A study of pupil, teacher and parent perceptions. *Research Papers in Education, 22*(3), 333–62.

Richards, M., Shipley, B., Fuhrer, R., & Wadsworth, M. E. J. (2004). Cognitive ability in childhood and cognitive decline in mid-life: longitudinal birth cohort study. *BMJ: British Medical Journal, 328*(7439), 552–54.

Richardson, K. (1999). *The making of intelligence.* London: Weidenfeld & Nicolson.

Rinaldi, C. (1998). The space of childhood. In G. Ceppi & M. Zini. (eds), *Children, spaces, relations: Metaproject for an environment for young children* (pp. 114–20). Reggio Emilia, Italy: Reggio Children and Domus Academy Research Centre.

Rinaldi, C. (2006). *In dialogue with Reggio Emilia.* London: Routledge.

Ritchey, P. N., & Fishbein, H. D. (2001). The lack of an association between adolescent friends' prejudices and stereotypes. *Merrill-Palmer Quarterly, 47*(2), 188–206.

Rodd, J. (1997). *Understanding young childrens' behaviours: A guide for early childhood professionals.* Allen & Unwin: Sydney.

Roffey, S. (2004). *The new teacher's survival guide to behaviour.* London: Paul Chapman.

Rosenfeld, A., & Wise, N. (2001). *The over-scheduled child: Avoiding the hyper-parenting trap.* New York: St. Martin's Griffin.

Rubin, J. L. (2003). No more junk toys: Rethinking children's gifts. *Mothering, 121*(Nov–Dec). Retrieved 6 December 2007, from http://www.mothering.com/articles/growing_child/consumerism/junk_toys.html

Rutledge, J. M., Topham, G. L., Kennedy, T. S., Page, M. C., Hubbs-Tait, L., & Harrist, A. W. (2007). Relation between parenting style and child weight. *FASEB Journal, 21*(5), A160–A165.

Sadker, D. (n.d.). *Some practical ideas for confronting curricular bias.* Retrieved 27 May 2008, from http://www.american.edu/sadker/curricularbias.htm

Saitz, R. (2006). Journal watch: pediatrics & adolescent medicine. Experience of child abuse and later perpetuation of violence. *Archives of Disease in Childhood, 91*(3), 274–75.

Sandstrom, M. J. (2007). A link between mothers' disciplinary strategies and children's relational aggression. *British Journal of Developmental Psychology, 25*(3), 399–407.

Schwebel, D. C. (2006). Safety on the playground: Mechanisms through which adult supervision might prevent child playground injury. *Journal of Clinical Psychology in Medical Settings, 13*(2), 135–43.

Schwebel, D. C., Summerlin, A. L., Bounds, M. L., & Morrongiello, B. A. (2006). The Stamp-in-Safety program: A behavioral intervention to reduce behaviors that can lead to unintentional playground injury in a preschool setting. *Journal of Pediatric Psychology, 31*(2), 152–62.

Schwichtenberg, A., & Poehlmann, J. (2007). Applied behaviour analysis: Does intervention intensity relate to family stressors and maternal well-being? *Journal of Intellectual Disability Research, 51*(8), 598–605.

Scull, A. T. (1977). Madness and segregative control: The rise of the insane asylum. *Social Problems, 24*(3), 337–51.

Sears, W., & Sears, M. (2002). *The fussy baby: How to bring out the best in your high-need child.* Illinois: La Leche League International.

Sears, W., & Sears, M. (2005). *The good behaviour book: How to have a better behaved child from birth to age ten.* London: Thorsons.

Seichepine, M. (2004). Childhood and innocence in Wuthering Heights. *Brontë Studies, 29*(3), 209–15.

Seo, K.-H., & Bruk., S. J. (2003). Promoting young children's mathematical learning through a new twist on homework. *Teaching Children Mathematics, 10*(1), 26–31.

Seskin, S., & Shamblin A. (2002). *Don't laugh at me.* Berkeley, CA: Tricycle Press.

Sharpe, M. N., York, J. L., & Knight, J. (1994). Effects of inclusion on academic performance of classmates without disabilities: A preliminary study. *Remedial and Special Education, 15*(5), 281–87.

Siegler, R. S. (1998). *Children's thinking* (3rd edn). Upper Saddle River, NJ: Prentice Hall.

Simplicio, J. (2005). Homework in the 21st century: The antiquated and ineffectual implementation of a time honored educational strategy. *Education, 126*(1), 138–42.

Skinner, B. F. (1953). *Science and human behavior.* USA: Simon & Schuster.

Skinner, B. F. (1987). What happened to psychology as the science of behavior? *American Psychologist, 42*(8), 780–86.

Skinner, B. F., & Ferster, C. B. (1957). *Schedules of reinforcement.* USA: Prentice Hall.

Sobsey, R. (2005, April). *Inclusive education research.* Presented at the Whole Schooling Conference 2005, Edmonton, Alberta.

Sook-Jung, L., & Young-Gil, C. (2007). Children's internet use in a family context: Influence on family relationships and parental mediation. *CyberPsychology & Behavior, 10*(5), 640–44.

South African Scout Association. (2003). *Extend your scouting: Scouting for the disabled* [Brochure]. South Africa: South African Scout Association. Retrieved 18 December 2007, from http://www.scouting.org.za/library/extendyourscouting/ExtendYourScouting.pdf

Spock, B. (1988). *Dr. Spock on parenting.* New York: Simon and Schuster.

Sprung, B. (2003). Young scientists at play. *Scholastic Parent & Child, 10*(6), 71–73.

Stager, G. (2006). Homework vs. the happy family. *District Administration, November.* Retrieved 1 October 2007, from www.districtadministration.com

Steinberg, L., Blatt-Eisengart, I., & Cauffman, E. (2006). Patterns of competence and adjustment among adolescents from authoritative, authoritarian, indulgent, and neglectful homes: a replication in a sample of serious juvenile offenders. *Journal of Research on Adolescence, 16*(1), 47–58.

Sternberg, R. J., & Berg, C. A. (1986). Quantitative integration: Definitions of intelligence: A comparison of the 1921 and 1986 symposia. In D. K. Detterman & R. J. Sternberg (eds), *What is intelligence? Contemporary viewpoints on its nature and definition* (pp. 154–63). New Jersey: Norwood.

Stratton-Lemieux, M. (2007). Fostering family literacy in ABC Head Start: The literacy backpack project. *Early Childhood Education, 37*(2), 22–28.

Straus, M. A. (1991). Discipline and deviance: Physical punishment of children and violence and other crime in adulthood. *Social Problems, 38*(2), 133–54.

Straus, M. A. (1994). *Beating the devil out of them: Corporal punishment in American families.* New York: Lexington Books.

Suzuki, M. (2008, January 15). Cellphones an 'obsession' for Japanese kids. *The Edmonton Journal,* p. A2.

Talking Tots. (n.d.). *Website.* Retrieved 16 October 2007, from http://www.talkingtots.info/

Tapp, J. L., & Kohlberg, L. (1971). Developing senses of law and legal justice. *Journal of Social Issues, 27*(2), 65–91.

Tarcov, N. (1984). *Locke's education for liberty.* Chicago: The University of Chicago Press.

Tarr, P. (2001). Aesthetic codes in early childhood classrooms: What art educators can learn from Reggio Emilia. *Art Education, 54*(1), 33–39.

Tarr, P. (2004). Consider the walls. *Young Children, 58*(3), 88–92.

Time Learning and Afterschool Taskforce. (2007). *A new day for learning.* Michigan: C. S. Mott Foundation. Retrieved 31 October 2007, from http://www.edutopia.org/pdfs/ANewDay-forLearning.pdf

Toomey, M. (1991). The price of masculinity based on violence. *Independent School, 51,* 41–43.

Trudgeon, C., & Carr, D. (2007). The impacts of home-based early behavioural intervention programmes on families of children with autism. *Journal of Applied Research in Intellectual Disabilities, 20*(4), 285–96.

Tucci, J., Mitchell, J., & Goddard, C. (2006). *Crossing the Line: Making the case for changing Australian laws about the physical punishment of children.* Victoria, Australia: Australian Childhood Foundation.

Turner, S. (2001). What is the problem with experts? *Social Studies of Science, 31*(1), 123–49.

Trost, K., Biesecker, G., Stattin, H., & Kerr, M. (2007). Not wanting parents' involvement: Sign of autonomy or sign of problems? *European Journal of Developmental Psychology, 4*(3), 314–31.

Truby, D. (2007). The well-organized classroom. *Instructor, 117*(2), 26–28.

Tsukakoshi, N. (2007). Preschoolers' understanding of wishing and magical events. *Japanese Journal of Developmental Psychology, 18*(1), 25–34.

Uditsky, B. (1993). From integration to inclusion: The Canadian experience. In R. Slee (ed.), *Is there a desk with my name on it? The politics of integration* (pp. 79–92). Washington, DC: Falmer Press.

Ulman, A., & Straus, M. A. (2003). Violence by children against mothers in relation to violence between parents and corporal punishment by parents. *Journal of Comparative Family Studies, 34*(1), 41–60.

UNESCO. (1995). Families and education. *Occasional Papers Series No. 18*. UNESCO. ERIC Document Reproduction Service ED397967.

United Kingdom Ministry of Education. (n.d.). *Equality*. Retrieved 25 May 2008, from http://www.teachernet.gov.uk/wholeschool/equality/

United Nations. (1959). *Declaration of the rights of the child*. Geneva: United Nations.

United Nations. (1989). *Convention on the rights of the child*. Geneva: United Nations.

Venville, G., Wallace, J., & Rennie, L. (2000). Bridging the boundaries of compartmentalised knowledge: Student learning in an integrated environment. *Research in Science & Technological Education, 18*(1), 23–35.

Victorian Curriculum and Assessment Authority. (2002). *Curriculum Standards Frameworks. Science. Level 6: Biological Science*. Melbourne: Victorian Curriculum and Assessment Authority. Retrieved 26 November 2007, from http://csf.vcaa.vic.edu.au/sc/loscbs06.htm

Victorian Institute of Teaching. (2007). *Draft code of conduct*. Melbourne: Victorian Institute of Teaching. Retrieved 13 November 2007, from http://www.vit.vic.edu.au/files/documents/1151_Draft-Code-of-Conduct_post-feedback.pdf

Vygotsky, L. (1978). *Mind in society: The development of higher psychological processes*. Cambridge, MA: Harvard University Press.

Walker, L. J. (1989). A longitudinal study of moral reasoning. *Child Development, 60*(1), 157–66.

Wall, R. (1987). Discovering prejudice against the disabled. *A Review of General Semantics, 44*(3), 236–39.

Wallingford, E. L., & Prout, H. T. (2000). The relationship of season of birth and special education referral. *Psychology in the Schools, 37*(4), 379–87.

Wang, Q. (2007). 'Remember when you got the big, big bulldozer?' Mother–child reminiscing over time and across cultures. *Social Cognition, 25*(4), 455–71.

Ward, L. (2006). High tech toys offer no educational gain, say researchers. *Guardian*. Retrieved 6 December 2007, from http://education.guardian.co.uk/elearning/story/0,,1947376,00.html

Wiechers, B., & Bester, D. (2006). How does the academic performance of South African home school learners compare to that of learners in state schools? *Tydskrif vir Geesteswetenskappe (Journal of Humanities), 46*(4), 456–67.

Wiggins, G., & McTighe, J. (2005). *Understanding by design* (2nd edn). Alexandria, VA: Association for Supervision & Curriculum Development.

Witt, S. D. (1997). Parental influence on children's socialization to gender roles. *Adolescence, 32* (126), 253–59.

Wong, H. K., & Wong, R. T. (1998). *The first days of school.* Mountain View, CA: Harry K. Wong Publications.

Woodard E. (2000). *Media in the home 2000: The fifth annual survey of parents and children.* Philadelphia: The Annenberg Public Policy Center of the University of Pennsylvania.

Wright, J. C., Huston, A. C., Murphy, K. C., St. Peters, M., Pinon, M., Scantlin, R., et al. (2001). The relations of early television viewing to school readiness and vocabulary of children from low-income families: The early window project. *Child Development, 72*(5), 1347–66.

Wulff, C. (2007). Violence and mass media: Are laws and regulations effective? *International Journal of Hygiene & Environmental Health, 210*(5), 547–50.

Yasemin, E. (2007). Sexism in school textbooks prepared under education reform in Turkey. *Journal for Critical Education Policy Studies, 5*(2), 15p.

Young, V. (1999). Revealing parenthoods: some observations on theoretical, lay and professional experiences of parenting in contemporary society. *Critical Public Health, 9*(1), 53–68.

Zlatka, C. (2007). Child's attachment to his/her mother, father and kindergarten teacher. *Early Child Development and Care, 177*(4), 349–68.

Zysk, M. B. (1999). *Homeschooling and the myth of socialization.* Retrieved 5 December 2007, from http://www.lewrockwell.com/orig/zysk1.html

Index